Toast the bards fae Blantir for their pc
Donate a quid to charity when you read the last two lines.
Thanks to Jimmy Whelan, Frank Devine and Thomas Slaven
And to all who went that extra mile with donations to The Haven.

(Extract from 'Los Crescentos')

Wan o the Flynns

Changing Places

By Frank Devine, Tom Slaven & Jimmy Whelan

Printed by Reid Printers, Blantyre
Published by Changing Places, Blantyre

ISBN 978-0-9570200-0-9

....

Preface:

I am pleased to write this preface
For poets of Blantyre, my native place,
Wherein three local men have made a start
To tell of the village, that's dear to their heart.

Jimmy, Frank and Tom to give them their name
Don't look for fortune, favour or acclaim
They want to make sure that in everyone's homes
There are people who want to read their poems.

All proceeds from sales according to Tom Slaven
Will go to a place that's called The Haven
A place of safety, that's simply divine
An idea proposed by Frank Devine

The input of this book by Jimmy Whelan
Is such that he's known as, "Jimmy the Wan".
This excellent idea from these three men
I recommend to you again and again.

So, I put pen to paper to endorse their view
In hope that their poems will indeed please you…

Enjoy the verse!

James Cornfield 2011

Foreword:

I am honoured, indeed, to have been asked to write an introduction to a fascinating book about the people and history of my birthplace of Blantyre. As far as my research has taken me, the first mention of the name 'Blantyre' (in its many variations), occurs in medieval times when the Prior of Blantyre Priory is recorded as attending a 'Parliament' at 'Briggenham' to discuss the betrothal of Princess Margaret of Scotland with Prince Edward of England.

Margaret, known as *The Maid of Norway* was the 11-year-old daughter of King Malcolm, and resident in Norway at that time. The Union never did take place, however. The Princess took ill on her sea journey and died of influenza before arrival in Scotland. The next factual record is when the Abbot of the Augustinian Canons Regular at Jedburgh Abbey was commanded at the behest of King Alexander 1 of Scotland to erect 'Rest Houses' at Blantyre, Forfar and Dumfries. The Abbot complied with the King's request, thus we in Blantyre have the remains of the Priory (now in ruins) which stood on a red sandstone Crag (Craig) on the Blantyre bank of the River Clyde opposite Bothwell Castle.

To Jimmy Whelan, Tom Slaven and Frank Devine I wish them all the best in their honest endeavours. I have no doubts that 'Parnassian Kings atop Mount Parnassus, home of poets, will acknowledge their ideas and enormous contribution in so many ways towards the formation of this book.

To the reader I recommend this book, not only on the content within, but with the knowledge that it is long overdue... I very much look forward to its publication.

James Cornfield 2011

Blantyre Poetry: *A Perspective by Frank Devine*

Introduction:

I have been allocated the pleasant and intellectually fulfilling task of recording the genesis, construction and completion of this anthology of Blantyre poetry. Contributing to this work is somewhat strange in itself for me, especially as I do not come from Blantyre and could be described by some from this fascinating village as a recent interloper (even although I have been here 12 years!).

But more importantly (and seriously), up until rather recently I have never had any particular interest in poetry. I am still not sold, as it were, on the poetry rationale, even as I pen these words as an introduction/contribution to an anthology of poetry (or verse, or whatever you might want to describe what will follow). Perhaps that is because I simply did/do not understand poetry? 'Poetry' was not 'for me' or 'my kind'. Or at least that is how I viewed poetry, and indeed, most forms of English literature, when I was growing up.

Why I felt uncomfortable about certain forms of the written word is somewhat strange because it did not apply to the written word per se only to 'poetry' and/or 'literature'.

Primary and secondary schools:

I have been a voracious reader since as far back as I can remember. While attending Holy Family Primary School in Mossend, I clearly recall my mum taking us as a family to Bellshill Public Library where I would 'make a beeline' for the small children's 'History' section and, at least as I remember, worked my way through the entire section (before moving on to the 'big' library. This interest in history stayed with me through my adolescent years as I retained an abiding interest in the subject, at least into my second year of study, at Our Lady's High School in Motherwell.

In point of fact, I don't really think this love of history ever left me, despite a process of degeneration kicking-in which coincided with large scale truancy which, to this day, I am still quite unable to explain. Despite passing the '11 plus' exam (which segregated children at 10 or 11 according to perceived educational or learning ability in those days), I left Our Lady's High School with no qualifications which, on reflection, must have been a source of huge embarrassment to my parents.

University 1:
Clydesdale Steel and Tube Works in Mossend:
After a number of short term jobs, my Dad (RIP), managed to get me into 'Stewart and Lloyds' (the company name before it was nationalised).
I remember my Dad telling me 'that's you made up now; a job for life'. Well, as a labourer, I never learnt much about the art of steel or tube-making but my reading skills improved exponentially. Day shift, back shift or night shift, what a library I was introduced into!

Despite coming from a devoutly Catholic background, I had developed into a hard-line socialist by this time (although my levels of commitment to the socialist ideal tended to fluctuate in line with other more materialistic pleasures and interests at various junctures in my life), but my reading tastes remained catholic in the universal sense of the word; The Daily Record, The Sun, Daily Mail, Daily Express, The Telegraph, Manchester Guardian (as it was then known), The 'London' Times, Morning Star, Socialist Worker and the various left-wing political newspapers which were doing the rounds in the early to mid 1980s. I also read stuff like Leon Uris' 'Trinity'; literature, of a kind, but I did not have 'that vocabulary' at this juncture in my life.

University 2:
University of Strathclyde in Glasgow:
After a fascinating year of studying social sciences at Motherwell College, I gained admittance to Strathclyde University from 1993-1997 and graduated with a BA (Hons), in Economic and Social History; and Politics. More importantly, Strathclyde University was a fantastic learning experience and introduced me to a far broader class, cultural, cosmopolitan and societal diversity than I had experienced up until that time.

Drinking in the Students' Union we would discuss our various subjects, tutorials, lectures and lecturers. Some of my best mates, in fact, almost all of them had a literature component as part of their degree and the names of (in no particular order), Robert Burns, Edwin Muir, Hugh MacDiarmid, Robert Crawford and Liz Lochhead began to enter my consciousness. The only Robert Service I had ever heard of was the historian; I was now aware of a poet of the same name, and a very famous poet at that.

University 3:

Blantyre:

I knew Jimmy Whelan long before I moved to Blantyre and soon got to know Tom Slaven (as well as hundreds of other people over this past 12 years!). As Jimmy Whelan commented at a meeting with Eddie Morrison (more of which later), 'we don't even drink together'- well, not usually! But it is a truism to state that we move in the same social circles in terms of politics, football and cultural matters. With the exception of the occasional pint (or two), the three of us, Tom, Jimmy and I, have been in touch via e-mail in relation to matters of mutual interest and concern for a fair number of years now.

About 2 years ago Jimmy began to post the occasional piece of poetry asking for my opinion. Why my opinion? I knew nothing about the damn stuff but felt obliged to peruse and give feedback, but more importantly, and despite myself, I began to enjoy reading the stuff. Jimmy also introduced me to some of the material being produced by not only himself and Tom Slaven but also by Brian Cummiskey, James Cornfield, Arlene McWilliam Green, Drew Semple and a number of others.

Changing Places:

I found this poetry or prose writing phenomenon amongst certain Blantyre people interesting on a number of levels. Firstly, I was beginning to enjoy reading poetry. I had never taken an interest in this sort of (for me anyway, abstract), writing in my life. And I was enjoying it.

Secondly, this was being produced by working class men and women who, for the most part, had not experienced a 'classical' introduction to literature in terms of a university education; that was how I thought people found out about poetry (Burns' was an aberration for me and did not register in my popular consciousness earlier for a number of cultural, social and political reasons). How wrong was I? I also at the same time suggested to Jimmy that it might be an idea to collate all of this stuff and perhaps publish it for charitable purposes. Unknown to me, Jimmy and Tom had already broached this subject so things appeared to be dovetailing in a positive direction. Thirdly, and most importantly of all, this poetry was clearly illustrating for me the concept of change within a community and specifically within the Blantyre community, a fundamental transition which really had served to alter that community out of all recognition in terms of lifestyles, incomes, popular pastimes, communal interests etc. But it was this process of transition that perhaps made this project all the more fundamentally important in terms of seeking to ensure publication, especially for the benefit of the present and future generations and as a fitting and important tribute to those who had gone before us.

The Haven Centre, Blantyre, Lanarkshire, Scotland: Caring, Counselling, Communication Centre:
There can hardly be a family in Scotland, which has not lost a relative to the curse of cancer. This horrendous disease affects tens of thousands of people in Scotland every year. There are a number of very caring organisations which have been established to assist people in coping with the consequences of this type of illness.

One such organisation is *The Haven* which is a registered charity which opened in Blantyre, Lanarkshire, Scotland in May 2002. Indeed, *The Haven* is a fantastic example of such an organisation and provides support to patients, carers and families affected by life-limiting illnesses such as cancer, Parkinson's Disease, Huntington's Disease, multiple sclerosis and to assist and help people to cope with the emotional, practical and psychological effects of such serious illnesses.

As well as also providing after-care to those who request it, individuals and families are able to self-refer to *The Haven* and its services are free and confidential. It should also be pointed out that, while *The Haven* is based in Blantyre, its services are available throughout Lanarkshire and beyond. The Haven is currently in the process of developing an outreach service for those who would rather avail of its services externally.

This wonderful organisation provides a holistic intervention in relation to the above issues and offers a multi-disciplinary approach to client care; complementary therapists, counsellors, volunteers, nurses and physiotherapists, all work together to ensure the most appropriate possible care is provided for its clients. Run by a 12 person board of directors, *The Haven* relies on funding from a variety of sources including The BIG Lottery Fund, various trusts, fundraising events and donations from the general public. And it is to raise much- needed funds for *The Haven* that the good ship *Changing Places* was set afloat.

The Collation of Works:
We (Jimmy, Tom and myself), were now in the process of collating poetry/verse/prose at quite an astonishing rate and from a wonderfully diverse number of contributors. These included various anecdotal and other testimonies written by a veritable genius on all aspects of local history in Blantyre, Jimmy Cornfield; a sprightly 80 year-old ex-miner and fire fighter who had long been an inspiration to many younger contributors to the book. Poetry/Verse began to arrive from such as Brian Cummiskey, Andy Downie, Arlene McWilliam Green, Marion Cummiskey Kane 1927-2002 (whose son gave us permission to include this fantastic women's prose in our book), Lon McIlwraith, Etta Gray Morrison, Paul Murray, Elizabeth 'Lizzie' Duddy Parry, Drew Semple and of course, Jimmy and Tom, all contributed some fantastic material to our proposed project.

Social Networking:
Social networking and our website have been fully exploited by the *Changing Places* project. *Changing Places* did, of course, require to be placed on a formal footing if we were going to move the project forward and succeed in sourcing funding for *The Haven* Charity. These issues were formalised with the inception of a fundraising arm which we incorporated within an excellent website we had established.

The Changing Places website would provide a paypal facility within which we would be able to solicit donations/sponsorship from members of the general public. Jimmy, Tom and I were extremely conscious that, the more we raised from public subscription the more we would be able to present to *The Haven*. Public subscription might provide the necessary funds for a first print-run of our book and this, if successful, would enable *Changing Places* to become self-financing and enable even more monies to be raised to go directly to *The Haven Centre*.

However, without question, it was the establishment of the *Changing Places facebook* page which was the catalyst for our fundraising. At the time of going to press, the *facebook* page had generated widespread interest not only in Blantyre but throughout Scotland, England and Ireland and, indeed, much further afield, including Australia and North America with more than 1500 members.

This page was fundamental to our fundraising project and assisted us very much in encouraging people to share anecdotes, pictures, videos and other interesting facts and features about growing up in industrial working-class communities throughout Scotland and indeed much further afield. The claim that *Changing Places* has served to bring the community of Blantyre together is incontrovertible.

Moving Forward:
I was in no position to provide a serious critical assessment of the poetic material submitted (although to be perfectly honest I was secretly delighted that Jimmy and Tom were sending me their work to comment on). It seemed to me (and both Jimmy and Tom agreed), that the best way to take our fledgling project forward was to take some of the writing into the local high school, John Ogilvie High School, to see if we could get an English teacher to have a look at the verse and provide some feedback for us in terms of its utility; are we wasting our time with this stuff, deluding ourselves or is there value and worth in what we were attempting to achieve in terms of presenting the collated work to a wider audience?

I duly presented the work to a Patricia Anderson who promised she would examine the verse and provide us with some feedback. I was, while somewhat apprehensive, delighted and fed this back to both Jimmy and Tom who must have felt the same as me. On the following Thursday I went to see Patricia who was clearly somewhat impressed with the work. Indeed, she informed us that the work had been passed to Eddie Morrison, Head Teacher of John Ogilvie High School (and a former English teacher), to comment on. Eddie asked if I could come and see him and he also commented that some of the material was very good, excellent even! Eddie indicated that he was interested in becoming involved in our fledgling project and a more formal meeting was organised.

We explained to Eddie what we were attempting to achieve in terms of the charitable dimensions of our project, asked him to comment on its usability, whether it would/could appeal to a wider audience. Eddie answered in the affirmative and from that time onwards began to (as indicated above), render sterling assistance to our project. Eddie suggested that we might also utilise the wonderful talents of some of his Senior pupils from the Art and Design Department within the school.

These outstanding young people were commissioned to provide illustrations that would reflect the area's rich industrial legacy and other aspects of the areas cultural, social and economic history. As such, *Changing Places* is indebted to the pupils of John Ogilvie High School who have provided the wonderfully evocative illustrations and art work which adorn this book. These were provided by Liam Burgess, Alix Cummiskey and Amanda Toms all of whom were delighted to be asked to contribute some of their fantastic work to this book.

Reamonn Gormley:
The truly outstanding contribution of the pupils of John Ogilvie High School has evidenced a truism which is much overlooked when some people comment on the nature of young people in contemporary society and the West of Scotland and Blantyre in particular.

The vast majority of our young people contribute positively to society and are at the forefront of seeking to assist those less well-off than themselves. And it is with this in mind that, while all monies raised by sponsorship/donations and purchase of *Changing Places* will be going to *The Haven Centre*, this book is being dedicated to the memory of Reamonn Gormley, an ex-pupil of John Ogilvie High School, who was brutally murdered whilst returning from watching his favourite football team in a local hotel.

Reamonn's all too short life illustrates for us all the goodness that can help to inspire other young people. Although an outstanding pupil at school and someone who gained immediate entrance into Glasgow University, Reamonn decided first to go to Thailand and participate in charity work with very disadvantaged school children (many with Down's Syndrome). It must have been all the more heartbreaking for his loving family and friends that it was on his return from making such a worthwhile contribution to those worse off in a material sense than any of us could probably ever imagine, that Reamonn's young life was to be so brutally cut short.

In the words of his former Head Teacher, Eddie Morrison;

"Notwithstanding the terrible loss of this young life, his death perhaps more than any other in Scotland, has served as a catalyst to our nation to face up to the cultural challenges which our communities must address in order to preserve all that is good and positive and cherished within our great country. It is a tremendous tribute to Reamonn and indeed to his family, that his death has made us realise as adults that we all have a responsibility to create communities that are safe and good and fit for our children. Blantyre has become something of a microcosm of our Scottish society and the significance of Reamonn's death has reverberated across every town and city of our nation. By dedicating this book to his memory, *Changing Places* has perhaps tried to acknowledge that".

Conclusion:
This book would never have come to fruition without the support and donations received from throughout the world but nowhere more so than from the community of Blantyre. We at *Changing Places* sincerely hope that you will enjoy this book in whichever way you feel suits your reading style. I would humbly suggest that it is certainly not a book to be rushed, rather one to be savoured, each and every word should be given time to sink into one's consciousness and should be read over and over again.

The book has been organised under a number of thematic groupings that may assist the reader find a particular area of interest. These are as follows: *Nostalgia; A Sense Of Place; The Price of Coal; Heroes and Demons; The Demon Drink*; and *A Sense Of Loss*. Hopefully the titles are self-evident.

Changing Places is an anthology of poetry that deserves to be passed down from generation to generation, of that I have no doubt. It deserves to be carefully preserved as an impressive document of a mining community before, during and after a process of fundamental transition which served to transform Blantyre and its environs forever.

We can only hope and pray that enough of the decent communal values and emphasis on social solidarity of those who have gone before us can be passed on by us to the coming generation. That, without question, must be the defining legacy of *Changing Places.*

Frank Devine 2011

Biographies of contributors:

James 'Jimmy' Cornfield:
Jimmy Cornfield was born in a famous mining part of Blantyre, known as Dixon's Rows, before moving to Logan Street in the village in 1932. Jimmy attended the local Saint Joseph's Primary School until the age of 14 when he started working on the pithead of the Bardykes Colliery (known locally in Blantyre as 'The Spittal'). Following conscription into the RAF in which he served for 3 years, Jimmy returned to work in Bardykes Colliery for a further period before joining the fire service where he served with three different regions: Lanarkshire, Glasgow and then Strathclyde until he retired in 1983 with the rank of station officer.

Jimmy was one of the 6 original members of the Blantyre Family History Group and is currently chairperson of the Blantyre Heritage Group. Jimmy is a noted expert on all aspects of Blantyre culture and its social, cultural and economic history, its people and place names and is forever on the lookout for more information on 'Blantir'.

Ann Crossar:
Anne Crossar was born in Beckford Lodge in Hamilton in February 1970. Anne's Dad was John and her mum was Cathie (nee Sim), Higgins. Ann attended St. Blanes' Primary School before going on to John Ogilvie High School in Hamilton. Ann was accepted into Strathclyde University and following graduation, has worked for South Lanarkshire Council as an Environmental Health Officer. Married to Ian Crossar from the village, Ann has 2 boys, Dominic and Johnny and, in her own words, loves her hometown of Blantyre and asserts that this is reflected in her family motto, 'Pro Patria' which means 'for the Homeland'.

Brian Cummiskey:
Brian was born to Alex and Alice (nee Brady), Cummiskey and is now in his 50th year. Brian now resides in East Kilbride but remains a 'Blantir' man through and through! Brian attended the local Saint Joseph's Primary School before going on to John Ogilvie High School in nearby Hamilton. Brian is a keen writer and poet and has had a number of works published in the local press. His first poem was titled 'Rosendale' and was written for his mother and father and referred to the tenement in Blantyre in which the family were

raised. Other poems Brian has written include, 'A Gentlemen's Distinction', 'A Plea for the Trees', 'Yer Fathers Old Books' and 'Dear John' about the actor John Hannah.

Frank Devine:
Frank was born in Glasgow on 14th January 1961 to Harry and Mary Teresa (nee Herron), Devine. Although both parents were of Irish stock or birth, Frank was raised in Mossend where he attended the local Holy Family Primary School and then Our Lady's High School in Motherwell. Frank eventually attended Strathclyde University in Glasgow and has now lived in Blantyre for 11 years. Frank has had a number of works of non-fiction published over the last 10-15 years. Frank is a member of Blantyre Heritage Group.

Andy Downie:
Andy was born on 7th August 1957 and has lived in Blantyre for the best part of his life and was the eldest son of Jimmy and Kathleen (nee McGuiness), Downie. Andy attended the local Saint Joseph's Primary School before going on to Holy Cross High School in Hamilton. Andy has been married to Marie since 1979 and has 2 daughters, Michelle and Sharon. In Andy's own words, 'I enjoy life to the full and have a fulfilling job. What I could not do without is my music and will continue to play guitar and sing 'badly' for as long as I can'. This is Andy's first published work in book form.

Mark (Mick/Boomer) Flynn:
Mick was born and bred in The Crescents district of Blantyre and has, more or less, with the exception of brief sojourns in Jersey and London, spent his life in the area. Born to Jimmy and Nancy (nee Casey) Flynn, Mick was educated at Saint Joseph's Primary School before going on to John Ogilvie High School. Coming from a family of 9 and with 4 children of his own, it might be reasonably assumed that Mick has never been fazed by interaction with others! This is Mick's first published work in book form.

Arlene McWilliam Green:
Arlene was born and bred in Blantyre and is the middle child of Bobby and Margaret (nee MacFarlane), McWilliam. After attending the local David Livingstone Primary School, Arlene went on to Blantyre High School then attended Bell College (now the Lanarkshire Campus of the University of the

West of Scotland), where she studied Applied Mathematics. It was while studying here that Arlene met her future husband and she has now been happily married to James for 20 years and they have 2 teenage daughters. Arlene loves to write poems and short stories but this is her first work to be published in book form.

Marion Cummiskey Kane 1927 - 2002:
Marion was born in 1927 to Michael and Margaret (nee McGrorty) Cummiskey and was raised in the Blantyre district. Marion married Dennis Kane in 1955 and had 3 sons and 1 daughter. However, it is believed by her surviving family that Marion started writing poetry sometime in the early 1950s following a short period of emigration to America (although her writing was unknown to her family at that time). Following marriage and the birth of her children, Marion joined a writers' group in Hamilton in the early 1970s and began to write poetry. One of her earliest pieces was believed to have been included in an edition of 'Irelands' Own', an extremely popular magazine amongst the Irish diaspora in Scotland and still widely bought to this day.

Marion self-published her own book of poetry in 1998 and was immensely proud that people took the time to read her work. Changing Places think it only right that contributions from this wonderful woman are included in this book and be recorded for posterity.

Lon McIlwraith:
Lon grew up in High Blantyre in the 1960s and attended High Blantyre Primary School and then Hamilton Academy (Grammar) until 1973. Lon's paternal grandfather was a coalminer in the Spittal Pit in Blantyre while his maternal grandparents owned 'Hastie's Farm Bar and Restaurant'; 'Hastie's Farm' was a popular venue in the local area renowned for its ability to attract some of the top artists of the day. Lon is a mechanical design engineer and now lives in Vancouver in Canada, but retains an abiding love of Blantyre and its people. Lon has had some of his work published on the Blantir's Ain website, but this is the first time his work has been published in book form.

Etta (Gray) Morrison:
Etta was born in Blantyre and lived at 1 Dixon Street (Dixon's Rows). Etta's mother was Nan Campbell and her father was Danny Gray who was a miner

in the local coalfield. Etta initially attended the local Auchinraith Primary School before moving on to Calder Street Secondary School in the village before going on to leave school at the age of 15. The inspiration for her poem, 'The Price of Coal' is said to have its origins in her childhood whilst being raised at Dixons Rows and the fear she felt when hearing the sound of 'the horn'. Etta's mother had instilled in her from a very young age that when 'the horn' sounded it signified disaster, death or serious injury to those men working below the ground.

Paul Murray:
Paul was born and bred in Blantyre in the mid 1960s. His father, Bill Murray, was also Blantyre-born while his mother, Bridie (nee Cullen), Murray, was raised in nearby Hamilton. Paul is a brother to both Carol and Stephen and all attended the local Saint Blane's Primary School and John Ogilvie High School in Hamilton. Paul's contribution to this book is his first published piece of work (indeed his first attempt at this sort of poetry) and he is very honoured indeed that his work has been included in this compilation.

James O'Donnelly:
James is a Blantyre man, born and bred, and was a son to John and Ellen (nee Kelly), O'Donnelly. James is one of eight children who were raised in the leafy suburb of 'The Crescents'. Although not a literary man, James could not escape folk, verse and song which were a constant presence in his house growing up, usually coming from the mouth of his 'mad mammy' (James's own words!). This background may well help to explain how he managed to contribute a poem for this collection. James is married to Jacqui and has three children at the local St Joseph's Primary School and John Ogilvie High School, the same schools he and his brothers attended. James is somewhat proud and even astonished that his work has been chosen for inclusion in a book for such a worthwhile cause.

Michael O'Donnelly:
Michael was born and bred in Blantyre and attended the local Saint Joseph's Primary School before going on to John Ogilvie High School. The youngest of John and Ellen (nee Kelly), O'Donnelly who had 8 children in total, his fondest memories are listening to his mother regale the family with stories of 'Old Blantyre' (and for Michael this constituted the pre 'Asda' era). Michael is looking forward to the day when he can share similar such stories with his own children.

Elizabeth 'Lizzie' Duddy Parry:
Lizzie was born and bred in the Blantyre area and was something of a philanthropist according to surviving members of her extended family. 'Lizzie' became a schoolteacher and throughout her life retained an abiding love of the written word and had a special gift for poetry.

Lizzie's only surviving poem that we have been able to trace at present is entitled, 'Each Bing a Headstone, Each Bing a Tomb' and tells the poignant story of her grandfather, Manus Duddy', who came to Scotland from Donegal in Ireland in 1887. It tells of the truly horrendous conditions experienced by miners and their families as they attempted to eke out a living in the Lanarkshire coalfield round about the 1890s – 1900s. This poem can truly be described as testament to the tens of thousands of other impoverished working-class families who endured such horrendous working, social and economic conditions at that time.

Drew Semple:
Drew was born in Bellshill on 11th September 1959. Drew's parents, Andrew and Mary (nee Thompson), were both from Blantyre and Drew was the youngest of 5 sons (2 of whom were, sadly, to die in infancy). Drew was raised in an area of Blantyre known locally as, The Orlettes' (temporary accommodation which was built to assist with the housing shortage in the area due to slum clearance and the destruction of the old 'Miners Rows'.) Drew attended High Blantyre Primary School and then went on to Calder Street School (later known as Blantyre High School). Drew is a keen local historian and singer/songwriter and has produced a DVD, 'Aint No Characters Anymore' (Story of Blantyre). Drew's DVD has been very successful and has sold over 2000 copies so far and can be purchased by contacting Drew on dsemple@blueyonder.co.uk

Thomas Slaven:
Thomas was born in Bellshill on 10th August 1966 and is the youngest of 3 children (Brother Patrick and Sister Margaret) born to Patrick and Catherine (nee Lynch), Slaven. Thomas was raised in the Coatshill area of Blantyre and attended the local Saint Joseph's Primary School before going on to John Ogilvie High School in nearby Hamilton. Thomas has developed a keen interest in poetry over this past number of years. This will be the first time his work has been published in book form.

James Joseph (Jimmy), Whelan:
Jimmy was born on 13th September 1966 to an Irish father and a Scottish mother, Thomas and Morag (nee Cummiskey) Whelan. Jimmy was born and bred in Blantyre and was the youngest of 3 brothers and attended the local Saint Joseph's Primary School before going on to John Ogilvie High School in Hamilton. Jimmy was fortunate to secure employment as an apprentice bricklayer and has followed that occupation ever since. Nevertheless, Jimmy has pursued his interest in the written word and earlier this year was the proud author of a privately published book of poetry, titled, *Verse About Life: (A Blantyre Boy).*

Contents:

Changing Places *(J.J. Whelan)*

Chapter 1 - Nostalgia:

You Can't Take the Man Out of the Street *(J. Cornfield)*
He Did It, I Saw Him *(D. Semple)*
The Great Rosendale Train Robbery *(B Cummiskey)*
Change *(J.J. Whelan)*
Boathouse *(J. Cornfield)*
Ma Coatshill Days *(T. Slaven)*
The Glesga Fair *(J.J. Whelan)*
I Think My Daddy Is A Vampire *(B. Cummiskey)*
A Big Day Oot *(Lon McIlwraith)*
Schools Oot *(J.J. Whelan)*
One Day *(T. Slaven)*
Summertime Blues *(J.J. Whelan)*
Up the Cauther *(B. Cummiskey)*
For the Better *(Drew Semple)*
Old Wreckers Ball *(B. Cummiskey)*
Fond Memories of Blantyre *(Ann Crossar)*
Aint No Characters Anymore *(Drew Semple)*
Broadway Train 1967 *(Lon McIlwraith)*
When I Was A Wean *(Drew Semple)*

Chapter 2 - A Sense of Place:

Blantir's Blood *(B. Cummiskey)*
Spirit of Blantyre *(A. McWilliam Green)*
A Poets Dream of Blantir *(J. Cornfield)*
Oor Toon *(J.J. Whelan)*
St. Joseph's Church *(J. Cornfield)*
The Crescents *(M. Flynn)*
Where Would I Be *(Andy Downie)*
The Dandy *(J. Cornfield)*

An Ode To the Blaneys *(A. Crossar)*
Blantir Way *(T. Slaven)*
The Blantyre Priory *(J. Cornfield)*
St. Josephs 1971-1978 *(J.J. Whelan)*
The Village People *(T. Slaven)*
Oor Ain Park *(D. Semple)*
The Call of Greenhall *(B. Cummiskey)*
Peter Craigs *(J.J. Whelan)*
Los Cresentos *(Wan a the Flynns)*
The Mill in The Meadow *(J. Cornfield)*
Owed to Facebook *(A. McWilliam Green)*

Chapter 3 - The Price of Coal:

Price of Coal *(E.M.Gray)*
Each Bing a Headstone, Each Bing a Tomb *(E. P. Duddy)*
The Rapper Up Man *(J. Cornfield)*
Spirit Among the Flame *(T. Slaven)*
A Breed Apart *(B. Cummiskey)*
Colliers Every Wan *(J. Cornfield)*
This Collier Breed *(J. Cornfield)*

Chapter 4 - Heroes and Demons:

The Blantyre Saint *(G. McLaughlan, Akn J. Cornfield)*
The Welfare *(J.J. Whelan)*
In the Footsteps of a Giant *(B. Cummiskey)*
The Wee God *(Lon Mc Ilwraith)*
Mr. Yuill and Dodds *(J. O'Donnelly)*
Reflections *(J.J. Whelan)*
The Boxer *(T. Slaven)*
The Meter Beater *(J.J. Whelan)*
Braw Broon *(Lon McIlwraith)*
Any Singers, Any Songs *(Anon)*
Fat Cats *(J.J. Whelan)*

Chapter 5 - The Demon Drink:

The Ballad of the Pale Rider *(B. Cummiskey)*
Blantyre's Boozers *(M. O'Donnelly)*
Bars and Superstars *(D. Semple)*
Sunday Morning Nightmare *(J.J. Whelan)*
Stagger 'Roon Blantyre *(Anon)*
Come Jine Me *(Lon McIlwraith)*
The Bingo Bungle *(Lon McIlwraith)*

Chapter 6 - A Sense of Loss:

To Reminisce *(T. Slaven)*
Faith *(J.J. Whelan)*
With the Brim of my Hat Turned Down *(M.C. Kane)*
The Last Song of the Lark *(P. Murray)*
American Dream *(J.J. Whelan)*
Forever In My Mind *(A. Downie)*
Guardian Angel *(J.J. Whelan)*
Seasons *(M.C. Kane)*
Absent Friends *(J.J. Whelan)*
Changing Places 2 *(J.J. Whelan)*

CHANGING PLACES (Blantyre)

When we strolled along the Auld Main Street
In the days of time gone by,
We always knew who we would meet
And the reasons why.

Now oor weans shuffle along the Auld Main Street
Heids doon and zippers high,
Terrified of who they might meet
And the reasons why.

J.J. Whelan

Nostalgia

Alix Cummiskey

YOU CAN'T TAKE THE MAN OUT OF THE STREET

As long as I live I'll never forget,
The day we were given a House to Let.
From Dixon's Rows on a horse and dray,
The Cornfield flittin' made its way,
Turning right at the shop of Annie C. Sweet,
Made its way up Logan Street.
The Street wherein the house
Is named after John Clark Forrest's spouce;
Janet Logan who died in her sleep,
Is immortalised by Logan Street.
The original families who came here,
Are in memory forever clear.
Their names keep running thru' my brain,
Let's see if I can remember them...
Dowdells, Cavanagh, Thomson, McSkimming;
Burt, Kelly, Chassels, Duffy;
McManus, McCorkindale, Bonnar, Carrol;
Murray, Neil, McInally, Corrigan;
Stoney, Rae, Wilson, Lynch;
Meechan, Paterson, Bailey, Millar;
Donnelly, Hailes, McGuire, Holmes;
McSorley, Torrance, Aitken, Ward;
Brown, Hill, Fullerton, Rodgers;
Middleton, Gibson, Cunning, Fitzpatrick;
Urbanski, Lennon, Reynolds, McInally;
Meechan, Tonner, Slaven, Cassidy;
Duffy, Marshall, McKenzie, Bordon;
Bailey, Chernouski, Waugh, Cornfield;
Boyd, McKee, Collins, Anderson;
Gibson, McGraw, Starrs, Taggart;
Marshall, Scullion, Rae, Duffy;
Paton, Cleary, Allan, Smith;
Hutcheson, McAlinden, Nicol, Montague;
Hoolahan, Scott, Nevins, Young.
Children with these family names,
Would meet in the street to play at games,
Lassies played Beds, Ropes and Ball,

Boys played Glessies, Headers and Football,
Run-sheep-run and Free the Den,
Nurkey-nurkey and Kick the Can,
Film-Star-Names, a Step for a Hint,
Hop-all-over, and your knees were skint.
If play had started, and you wanted a game,
You always asked for a Cock or a Hen.
The games we played one after another,
Seemed to last forever and ever.
We played all day till we heard the shout,
"Come in, come in, your tea is out!"
Best of all was a great big slide,
At the top of the Street where nobody styed.
Then we came out when it was night,
And sat below the Lampost's light,
Telling stories that made us scared,
To go home in the dark, cos we were feart.
We all held hands with one another,
Making sure we went home together,
Then off to bed to dream our dreams,
And rise tomorrow and play our games.
The street was busy in those far-off days,
People from all over came our way:
Blin' Watty, Cheap Johnny, the Old Co-op van,
Alex Kerr, the shilling-a-week man,
Wee Dom the Tally the Ice Cream man,
Johnny 'the Darkie' with case in hand,
Jenny the Pack, the Provident man,
Mr John Graham the Preacher man.
Wullie Tonner, mouthpiece and clappers,
Playing tunes that drove us crackers,
A Blin' man who sang like a Linnet,
The sent his pal round with the Bunnet.
Strooling Minstrells from all the Airts,
Men selling fruit from open Cairts.
They all sang for their daily bread,
Any song for a Penny could be heard.
Every Saturday at the 'Doocot',
For entertainment you couldnae whack it;

Robin of Sherwood was Errol Flynn,
Chief Crazy Horse was Anthony Quinn,
Johnny Mack Brown shot all the bad yins,
Especially if they were Red Indians.
Whatever the picture, we all made a din,
A Penny or Jeely Jar got you in.
I went back down there the other day,
Jist to let my memory stray,
Taking some photos here and there,
When all at once I was aware,
Of some wee boys following me,
Jist like the boys of Logan Street dae.
Looking and at the same time saying,
"Haw Mister whit are ye dae'in?"
Cheeky wee faces looked up at me,
Among them the boy that once was me,
My pals and I were standing there,
Faces from the past some no longer here,
We asked the same as these wee boys do,
"Haw Mister who ur you?"
Long years may pass, yet still remain,
No change at all, it's jist the same.
This then was oor Logan Street,
A magic place where weans could meet.
Go up the Calder or down the Clyde,
Or slide down the Bing on your backside.
It did'nt matter what we done,
We always seemed to have such fun,
Childhood days within the scheme,
Memories Golden and Evergreen. . .

James Cornfield 2005

HE DID IT! I SAW HIM!

We aw know a man who saw a dinosaur
Or a man who saw a shark
Or a man who saw an alien
Or a ghost comin oot fae the dark.

Ask Oor Jake cause he was there.
We saw the white lady wae straggly hair
We started to run, but she could fly,
And oan her broom she passed us by-
A saw her!!

She picked us up and drapped us aff
At Davy Livvies brig.
She drapped us aff just in time
To start oor next gig.

We met the troops we told them
Exactly what we saw-
When a killer whale came oot the Clyde
And punched me oan the jaw-
Jake saw it!!

His stories are daft but are they true?
Just ask ma brither, cause he saw them too!

Just at that I drapped a pound
Doon intae the watter.
Then Oor Jake turned and said,
"Heybro, it diznae matter!"

He promptly did a swallow dive
Doon intae the Clyde.
He got ma pound and soakin wet
He's standin by ma side-
A saw him!!

Just at that a Viking ship
Came sailing roon the bend,
Loaded wae big mad Vikings
A thought that wiz the end!

But oor Jake shouted "Square go"
I'll fight yeez wan by wan!
Ye don't know who yer dealin wi
Cause I'm a Blantir man!"
A heard him!!

He battered aw the Vikings
And set the ship alight.
Oor Jake was still upright
after such a fight-
Jake did it!!

A saw him!!

Drew Semple

THE GREAT ROSENDALE TRAIN ROBBERY

Ma favourite toy when as wis wee
Wis a big red plastic train.
Ah big boy stole it affy me,
And it wis never seen again.
Ah wonder if he remembers
That favourite toy of mine?
Ah wonder if he's in prison now
Remembering his very first crime?

Brian Cummiskey

Alix Cummiskey

CHANGE

We often feel the need for change
As we say it's as good as a rest,
But we often fail to stop and wonder
If change is for the best.

Sometimes we change too many things
In a way, a shape or form
When a constant need for change occurs
Then change becomes the norm.

We decide to change the décor
In fear our rooms have faded.
Yet when we change the wallpaper
Our furniture looks jaded!

Now change can become our mentor
As change succeeds each change.
Every time you look at something
The unchanged seems strange.

So, if you feel you're sorely tempted
To enforce some unneeded change,
Just change your mind and stop and think
Don't change it, for a change.

J.J. Whelan

BOATHOUSE, BLANTYRE

Twixt Calder and Clyde, near Haughead,
Is where our native people did tread.
As did a man by the name of Blane,
Who once passed by and left us his name.

Thru' the mists of time of reverie,
I hear again this plaintive plea
Of voices calling for the ferry boat,
" Bo-at Jock! Bo-at Jock! "

Just like mystical Brigadoon ,
Boathouse appears from within the gloom,
As once again I turn and see,
This ancient site near Blantyre Priory.

The call is heard inside the cottage,
By the Ferryman whilst at his pottage,
Who rising swiftly from his chair,
Makes haste towards the small pier. . .

To where his Skiff is safely moored.
Making sure it's properly oared,
He launches forth onto the Clyde,
And rows toward the other side.

To ferry travellers to and fro,
Is the job of Hie'lander John Munro,
At which task he is the best,
Being strong of arm and broad of chest.

I stood there as if hypnotised,
At the event taking place before my eyes.
Then reality returned to this old place,
Whilst I walked on at thoughtful pace

This really did happen of that I'm sure,
But then again I'm not too sure.
If like Brig-a-doon it should appear,
Then again I'll have no fear.
For it only happens every hundred years. . .
Or does it ?. . .

James Cornfield 2008

MA COATSHILL DAYS

Doon Coatshill was where I was raised
I'll never forget those happy days,
Playin ower the dump a game of crossie
In sunshine or rain and even when froastie.

Doon Davy Livvies red ash park on a Sunday
Twenty a side, we could o' played tae the Monday,
Ten hauf -time and twenty-wan-the-winner!
Then up the road fur yer Sunday dinner.

Intae ma wee hoose at 6 Morven Lane
Lie on the couch with ma legs in pain,
As Ma Mammy worked her culinary magic
I'd set the table then listen to life's logic.

Coatshill had loads of really great people
In every hoose and under the steeple.
Always there tae help the lost and the needy
An' ye aye goat pelters if they thought you were greedy.

In the long summer days, games of Wan Man
They'd last aw night, well, that wiz the plan.
Nae School the morra , ya beauty!– stay oot late
Ma Coatshill days wur truly great!

Tom Slaven

THE GLESGA FAIR

Well aff we went on our annual crusade,
Away oer tae Rothesay, wae oor buckets and spades.
We set aff fae Blantyre, away tae Wymess Bay
Praying we could keep the (ticket) inspector away.

I stood at the jetty looking in awe,
At this massive big ship that would take us awa'.
I stood at the bow like Jack in Titanic,
But there was nae Rose fur me, just ma maw in a panic.

We hurried aff the gangway oan tae dry land,
There was nae time tae stop or tae take anybody's hand.
Up tae the digs we would venture,
One bedroom flat. Nine of us, now that wiz an adventure!
On to the beach we would go,
Running intae the water, that was four below.
Oor parents would sit there, wae their wee carry oot,
Watching the weans gaun in fur a dook.

The fortnight was spent, fishing and putting,
It's the aw ye could dae, cause ye got it fur nothing.
We had fish every night, 'cause we got it fur free,
Sunday, ma Granny, off tae the Glenburn for a spot of high tea.

Now if we were good we would aw' get a treat,
Zavaroni's for aw' the ice cream you could eat.
On to the Winter Gardens for a shot oan the shows,
Oh how good those days were, evrywan knows.
I have such wonderful memories there,
'Specially of "The Glesga Fair."

J.J. Whelan

I THINK MA DADDY IS A VAMPIRE

I think ma daddy is a vampire,
Because he only goes oot at night.
He looks like Bela Lugosi
And his hair is black and white.

I think ma daddy is a vampire,
He's become one of the great un-dead,
And he shouts:
"A'm oan the night shift
Ah need tae get tae ma bed."

I think ma daddy is a vampire,
Who came from old Blantyre.
His mum and dad own a castle there
It's got a ghost and a big gas fire.

So if you think your daddy is a vampire
Who looks like Christopher Lee:
Remember he works the night shift,
So please let that vampire be.

Brian Cummiskey

Amanda Toms

A BIG DAY OOT

Two wee boys went oot wan day,
As wis their usual fancy,
By the church and on their way,
Towards the Lady Nancy.

They steppit oot across the fields,
They scaled the farmer's fences,
The cows got up and chased their heels,
The boys escaped by inches.

Up they climbed the gorsey cap,
Aw scratched and scraped all over,
Then spied upon the grassy tap. . .
A pair of nudie lovers!

Doon they fell tae keep unseen,
Then keekin' through the branches,
Wi' gapin' gobs and poppin' een,
They stared as though in trances.

The lovers lay tae catch the sun,
They didnae move a muscle,
Thinkin' they were aw alone,
Away fae aw the bustle.

But then the wee boys broke the spell,
They burstit oot in sniggers!
The man jumped up, let oot a yell!
The wuman reached for covers.

Off the pair ran though the gorse,
In laughin', roarin' fettle,
The man gave chase, but came off worse,
He wisnae dressed for nettles!

Doon the boys ran back that day,
Through fields and cows and fences,
By the church and on their way,
Wi' tales of Lady Nancy.

Lon McIlwraith

SCHOOLS OOT

When we were wee we had such fun
Playing kerby and chap door run,
Kick the can and best man fall,
Playing rounders and kicking a ball.

We'd go up the Cauther or doon the Clyde,
Fair Monday, we're off tae the seaside.
Going for runs on your Chopper bike,
Motherwell boating-pond fishing for pike.

We'd go tae the Dandy or the Army Camps
Swim in the Quarry, in oor pants.
Away to the Priory hunting for rabbits
Following our elders, picking up bad habits.

We'd make great bogies fae auld prams
Assembling them, as fast as we can.
Tae the top of the street we'd run
The harder the shove, the more rubber we'd burn.

We'd be eating pieces on Strawberry jam
If you were posh, you would have Spam!
Eating fresh rhubarb with sugar in a poke
Upset stomach, it gied ye the boke.

We'd be up the Bing, "Breed Boards" in place,
Downhill racing, at such great pace!
Hame to your mother, she'd hiv a fit
You looked as though, you'd crawled oot the pit!

We'd often get caught being up tae nae good
Hame wae the Polis, tae bed wae nae food,
A whack wae the slipper and a stern telling aff
Another adventure, whit a great laugh!

People might say we had a misspent youth
We'll tell you, we were just misunderstood.
We had so much fun in those school's oot days
And the days may be gone but their memories stay.

J.J. Whelan

ONE DAY. . .

One day, I'd like to see friendship for all
In a community where we all stand tall.
We need the spirit of, "we're all in it together"
On the banks of the Clyde and purple heather.

One day, not far, I'd like to hear
That our community can live without fear.
We can enjoy a walk or bleather on oor streets
No need for fear of the strangers we greet.

One day, I hope we can all feel safe
As we welcome the poor, the needy, the waif
To this lovely town and its great people
Where all live together under one steeple.

One day, I hope we can taste victory
As we take our place in Blantir's history,
And know we helped change our town for the good
To a place where all are truly understood.

Tom Slaven

SUMMERTIME BLUES

With the grass so green
And the sun so bright,
I watch the flowers
Bloom with delight.

Kids with ice cream
Their smiling faces,
T- Shirts and tans
Folks with red faces.

Paddlin' pools
Laughter and joy,
Kids so happy
Playing with their toys.

Children with camps
From branches and trees,
Playing football a' night
Going home with skint knees.

Summer sleepovers
Staying with friends,
Barbecues and drinks
Summer night never ends.

Then the sun gets lower
The leaves start to fall,
Such a short summertime
Oh how we'll miss it all. . .

J.J. Whelan

UP THE CAUTHER

Up the Cauther oan a Summer's day,
Cummiskeys and Whelans came oot tae play;
Up for a Dook in the manky watter
Then listen tae Tam 'n' Morag's patter.

The whole of Blantir seemed tae be there
Especially during the Glesca Fair.
Aunties, Uncles, Cousins all,
Up the Cauther hivin' a ball.

Hankies own heids, big red faces,
Troosers rolled up, string vests an' braces.
Blantir Barneys were everywhere,
Oot for the day in their underwear.

Tryin' tae catch baggie's wae yer wee green net,
Playin' tig an always being het;
Watching the boys divin' aff the falls,
Wae their cut up jeans 'n' Tarzan calls.

I still recall those golden days,
Up the Cauther in the sunny haze;
I still see the faces, I still hear the patter,
When we went for dooks in the manky watter.

I sit here now by clearer water,
Beside me sits my sons and daughter;
And I tell them of a summer's day,
When Cummiskeys an' Whelans came oot tae play.

Brian Cummiskey

THE BIG FIGHT

"Doon the park efter school!
You're deed!" That's the rule.
Nae gone tae the Jannie
Or telling yer Mammy,
Nae big brithers
Or help fae others.
Just you and me, square go.
Nae punchin doon below,
Nae scratchin, nae biting
Only good clean fighting.

The haunshakes are done,
The fight has begun,
The first punch is threw,
And the air is punched blue,
Not a blow has been struck,
As the grun turns to muck,
Their claes are awe manky,
Oot comes the hanky,
They call it a draw,
And run hame tae their Maw.

J.J. Whelan

FOR THE BETTER

The streets are so much wider now
The tram cars are all gone.
The sandstones lost the battle
To the supermarket spawn.

Stonefield Road was vibrant
The shops had cake and candy
You crossed the road to go a walk
And headed down the Dandy.

The public park gala day
Was a sight to behold.
Logan Street, Elm street
These were Streets of gold.

Regeneration, modernisation
The answer to it all .
We took their word for gospel
As we watch our last school fall.

"This is for the better."
They told our parents then.
This is for the better?
When?

Drew Semple

THE OLD WRECKERS BALL

Corsairs and Zephyrs were piled high
Once proud cars. . . That caught your eye
Their former glory turned to rust
As they gathered amongst the dust.

The wreck of a Ford Cortina
Its paintwork all flaked away,
Sat beside a Vauxhall Victor
In the fading light of day.

Austin vans with windows smashed
Ford Anglias interiors slashed.
A Jaguar that has seen better days
All broken. . . in a dusty haze.
Imps and Beetles, Hunters too,
A Humber Hawk, painted blue
All waiting their turn in the queue.

The king of the road had come to die
Their headlights reaching for the sky.
Taken to their final rest
By the owners who knew. . . they were past their best.
A real sad sight, it filled your eyes
To see those cars with a rusty disguise,
Gathered there. . . One and all
Piled high at the "Old Wreckers Ball".

Brian Cummiskey

FOND MEMORIES OF BLANTYRE

A quaint little mining village in the heart of Lanarkshire
Is the town I hold dearly, my hometown of Blantyre.
The cotton mills long closed and the mines are long gone
But the town remains famous – thanks to our own David Livingstone.

Growing up in the Tyre was a wonderful education,
A "University of Life" to handle any situation.
"Being prepared" in the Brownies or tap dancing at Ms Roxburgh's
Scouts or Football for the boys – all our needs were catered for.

Buying your weekly groceries in Templetons Supermarket
Or a shag pile for your living room from McIntosh Carpet.
Stepek each month to rent out your colour telly,
Gala Days in the summer thanks to the Miners Welly!

Two discos in the town – there was Zeigfields and there was Caspers,
Ladies clothing taken care of courtesy of clothes shop named Rapture.
Lightbody's chip buttie was always a delicious treat
Mauchline's newsagents for their fabulous trays of sweet.

The Speedway in the town, an attraction for some.
Market Day on a Tuesday was always such fun.
Papa Franks, and the fabulous disco floor
The Manhattan on a Saturday was worth waiting for.

The Public Park so immaculate with its beautiful flower beds
Getting your clubs for the putting from 'the wee man in the shed'.
"Come in Number 6" was the shout from the boating pond.
Families having fun in the wonderful parkland.

Pubs closing early for a few hours on a Sunday
Nothing else for it – a short stroll down to the Stanley.
The Commercials sing-a-long and Delilah by Ed
Functions in the Parkville – looked after by Ned

YMCA discos and the Lizzie Scott Playscheme
Blantyre Vics and the Celtic – our very own football teams.
The Snooker Club on a Sunday for a big game of killer,
Barnums and the Red Lion for a cool bottle of Miller!

Queuing for hours to get into the new swimming pool
A mars and ice from Mickey's cafe in the summer to keep us cool.
Quiznight in Teddies organised by quizmaster Jeff Pate!!
A trip down to Davy Livvies in the summer was great.

A walk up the "cawther" to catch some wee baggie minnows,
The video shop on Stonefield to rent your betamax videos.
Jock Richardson's for your sausage – was it square or was it link?
The bestest people in the World – well that's what I think!

Yes such fond memories growing up in my hometown of Blantyre
This quaint little mining village in the heart of Lanarkshire

Ann Crossar

AINT NO CHARACTERS ANYMORE

O'er the park fur a gemme o' shoots,
Ma maw bought me fitba boots.
Oot o tandem or matt the poles,
Put the jaikets ahint the goals.
They were Celtic, we were the Rangers,
In those days there were no strangers.
Those days are gone and the pain is sore.
Aint no characters anymore.

Doon the prefabs up the bing,
O'er the cawther tae make a swing.
Doon tae Vinsie's tae get a chip,
Walkin hame ye got nae lip.
Went tae the Broadway once or twice
Then tae Mickey's fur a mars and ice.
Those days are gone and the pain is sore.
Aint no characters anymore.

I miss the old days,
The old ways and the suns rays.
I miss my old mates,
White gates and Wullie Pates.
Remember Nessie's, The Cosy and Rosendale?
Davy Livvies, Battersie's fur a pun o nails?
Born in the Orlettes among the guid folk,
When aw the punters could take a wee joke.

O'er tae McVey's tae huv a beer,
Walkin hame there was nae fear.
But now they say that life's a bore.
There aint no characters anymore.

Drew Semple

BROADWAY TRAIN, 1967

Oor Mum gave us a ten bob note,
Tae see the Saturday mat'nee,
So me an' ma wee sis and bro,
Went aff tae the Blantyre Broadway.

It wis sae nice, the summer heat,
We'd raither be ootdoors insteid,
Then walkin' doon Victoria Street,
An idea came intae ma heid.

We'd get oorsels aboard the train,
Fae Blantyre tae Glasgow Central,
A rerr day oot for us three weans,
And oor Mum wid never tipple.

Ah telt this plan tae ma wee crew,
Ma wee brother thought it wis grand,
Wee sister wisnae quite sae sure,
But she said okay in the end.

We bought some sweeties fae a shop,
Tae begin oor big adventure,
Then quick we flew, a skip and hop,
Straight past the Broadway pictures.

But haufway doon auld Station Road,
Wee sister she burst oot greetin',
The tears they flowed and froze she stood,
Despite oor soothin' and pleadin'.

Ah said tae her, "C'mon noo sis,
Oor Grampa takes us tae the toon!"
Ah held her haun, gave her a kiss,
And whistled a wee Grampa tune.

That wis just the thing she needed,
Tae put aff her apprehension,
And oor wee gang then proceeded,
Tae the Blantyre railway station.
Ah gave ma best big brother face,
For the man ahint the wicket,
"Three cheap returns please, toon's the place,"
And wi' that we had oor tickets.

The train came soon alang the line,
And stopped wi' a screech and rattle,
Ma heartbeat fluttered, like a sign,
As we barged on in a prattle.

The carriage lurched, gave a shudder,
When the train man blew his whistle,
Moved slowly first, then much quicker,
Pulled by the noisy big diesel.

Newton we passed, then Cambuslang,
We were wide-eyed in sensation,
The railway tracks a-rat-tat sang,
As we neared the Central Station.

The train slowed doon, a sudden halt,
But we didnae hit the buffers,
Off we got in that mockit vault,
Made black by the auld steam puffers.

Just we three, in crowds of people,
Their wee hauns Ah held sae tightly,
Ah stretchit tall, like a steeple,
But could see the boards just slightly.

Wee sis and bro, excited noo,
Were askin' too mony questions,
Ah answered them as best Ah knew,
Zig-zaggin' through the congestion.

"Look way up there," Ah said oot loud,
"D'ye see that, platform seven?
That train'll take us oot this crowd,
And back tae the Blantyre station."

So fast it seemed, the back-hame train,
Wi' relief Ah steppit aff it,
We crossed the bridge, went up the lane,
And the long walk hame wis startit.
The two wee wans were tickled pink,
Their day oot had been a riot,
But walkin' back Ah had tae think,
How tae make them keep it quiet.

"Listen youse two, we had great fun,
But we cannae let mummy know,
So if she asks us whit we've done,
We'll say a Broadway movie show."

Mony years later, Mum wis told,
The big secret we'd kept sae well,
She said she knew, but didnae scold,
She'd done the same thing twice hersel.

Lon McIlwraith

WHEN I WIS A WEAN

Meccano sets or Johnie 7
The toys that made a boy in heaven.
Cheesecloth shirts and two bob chain
Those were the days when I was a wean.

Platform shoes and crombie jacket
Bought wi a provie line, cost me a packet.
Working class da, working class maw
Took me to Brownlees to buy me a baw.

Our only phone was doon the stair
A party line we had to share.
We let our pals in, just to see
Our state of the art, black n white TV.

The Dandy, The Beano, or maybe the Topper
Bazooka Joe chewing gum or even a whopper.
To the record session everybody went
Playing daft games like Nervous or Content?

Dial-a-disc or the speaking clock
Playing at beds marked oot wi chalk.
I'd give up everything to do it again
Those were the days when I was a wean.

Drew Semple

A Sense of Place

Original carvings by Tommy Hawkins

BLANTIR'S BLOOD

There's nae where else like Blantyre,
Its people are a breed apart.
Some of us love its history,
Others its streets and art.
No matter where ye wander,
Blantyre's still in you.
No matter where ye live in this world,
Yer Blantir' through and through.

Brian Cummiskey

THE SPIRIT OF BLANTYRE

From the heights of Auchentibber
Rolling down to the Clyde,
Nestles our fair town
For which I'm full of pride.

It has history and passion
A story great to tell,
Of miners who toiled
And of many who fell.

Of World War One heroes
The sons of long ago,
Of a famous explorer
Who to Africa did go.

Of the Priory where once
The holy men would pray.
Old churches and chapels
Still grand to this day.

The Clyde and the Calder
That flow through the town,
The Pech Brae that you can't run up
But can always run down.

My family of old
Grew up on these streets,
And of the town and its history
Lessons they'd teach.

Of hardworking people
Who knew how to survive,
Who through wars and strikes
Kept their spirits alive.

The people of Blantyre
Know how to laugh and to cry
Stand up all our townsfolk!
Proud to be one am I!

Arlene McWilliam Green

A POET'S DREAM OF BLANTIR

When man, by fate or feelings of heart,
Roams upon some lonely moor apart,
At twilight, when silence reigns supreme,
He muses long, neath moonlight beam.

On such a night, I wander forth
To Blantir Woods where the Clyde flows thru.
O`er Dandy Brig I wend my way
As lengthening shadows hail end of day.

All o`er the scene, contentment rests,
As feelings rise within my breast.
As here and there, I cast a roving e`ee
At nature's beauty one can see.

A host of Bluebells o`er banking spread,
The leafy bower entwines o`erhead.
And feathered things, full blithe their song
Echo the roving wildwoods throng.

The briar rose glistens midst the green,
Its lovely blossom like some jewel is seen.
Thro` Jolly's garden I make my way,
Not known as Jolly's nowadays.

I aimlessly stray thro` flowery dell,
As Bothwell bells, the hour dost knell.
The night is fine, with stars a-shining,
A braw full moon is upwards climbing.

The Shuttle Row on yonder hill,
Stands out, now dark and strangely still,
Where Livingstone, the Christ in man,
Sprang forth thru` God's creative plan.

Every man, tho` he roams this earth,
Aye hankers for his place of birth.
Thru` aged dimmed eyes, he'll view with joy,
The place he loved and becomes the boy. . .

Who barefoot ran thru` Blantir`s braes,
And swam the Clyde in childhood days
To eat the fruit from yonder trees,
In Blantir`s ruined, old Priory.

Where Clyde and Calder come to meet
Tis` here you'll find a place so sweet.
A priest among men, by the name of Blane,
Came from afar and left us his name.

A poem by Wullie Sharp.
(Edited and amended by James Cornfield, Blantyre Heritage Group – June 2004)

OOR TOON

Made in Scotland from Irish stock
Blantyre's where I cut my teeth.
Where boys were boys and men were men
Wae Potted Heid and Corned Beef.

The Bowling Alley, Wullie Pates,
Harpers Garage and Matt the Poles,
Mars on Ice at Mickey's Cafe
Peter Craig's and Little's rolls.

Playing at fitba doon the park
Trying to live the dream
A Wembley Trophy and jaickets for goalposts
Scoring the winner for your favourite team.

Such a lovely quaint wee place
I love and know so well.
As time has passed it has changed
For the good? Only time will tell...

J.J. Whelan

ST. JOSEPH'S CHURCH

St Joseph's Church, you bear the name of a gentle saint.
You've been here one hundred years with thee we are acquaint.
Should we go back in time, `til the moment thou came to be,
We would surely find the man whose only dream was thee.

The Rev. Thomas Hackett, the doctor who made thee his quest,
Told the Glasgow Archdiocese, "For Blantyre it's only the best".
This man of God tho` small in stature was very big in faith
And never took no for an answer as long as he could breathe.

He informed the family Pugin, church builders of renown
A lovely church in gothic style, to be built of red sandstone.
John Aitkenhead then built thee, on the site the Doctor chose
As soon as thy walls began to rise, the problems then arose.

Protestors and there were many, vandalised the work being done.
They went on to the site at midnight and knocked every stone.
The thought that a Catholic Church would again in Blantyre reign,
Drove them to such terrible acts, their deeds were done in vain.

Some Irish Catholic miners "The Chapel Gate Crowd" by name,
Volunteered to watch o`er thee, guardian angels they became.
From dawn `til dawn o`er three long years, vigilant and proud
These brave men protected thee, from this unholy crowd.

With every day that passed, like the phoenix you arose
From the ashes of the priory, to the place midst miners rows.
Built as you are next to Livingstone Church, created a lovely story
Mayberry Place the building between, became known as Purgatory.

Majestic house of God, how shall we extol thee?
Of all Blantyre Churches, thou are the fairest one can see.
None can compare with thy elegance, grace and beauty
To make good the Doctors work, Parish Priests have made their duty.

To maintain, nay to improve thee, has always been their aim,
With donations from our forebears, Colliers and Weavers by name.
Who gave their hard-earned coppers, towards thy building fund
And made the doctors dream come true, a house for God's own Son.

Tis` here he dwells the Son of God, within a tabernacle
To twelve apostles he then explained the great miracle.
The mystery of the Last Supper of the bread and of the wine
Then told these twelve disciples to go forth and preach divine.

Today we pay thee homage as we come to celebrate
A century of Prayer, Faith and Worship within thy holy estate.
May we, as in those days of yore, when thou came to this earth,
Be worthy of God's Blessing as we commemorate thy birth.

James Cornfield 2005

THE CRESCENTS

Choose the right exit off Victoria Street
An' the folks who you meet there are really unique.
There's polis an' nurses an' mathematicians
An' clergy who'd forgive you for An Act of Contrition.

In the summer the swingy's, where we'd watch Punch and Judy
Glen Michael's cavalcade wae yon mad dug, Rudy.
Brian Connolly from "Sweet" came, but left in a hurry
Wae a face full of lipstick from the bold Miss Murray.

The corner was where all the action was at
Wae the legend James Meechan, king of the chat.
He once snecked Liz Taylor an' denied it was pleasant
But not the same one who lived in Small Crescent.

'Toni the Tally', with his magical chimes
Who would say. . ." You a frosho". . . just a couple of times?
Huntin' for gless cheques to spend at the van
Then Grand National over hedges, we laughed as we ran.

The McLeans & McAdams were Sunday best players
In their Arthur Black shirts an' high waist bands wae flairs.
Their diving heeders were elegant, their scissor kicks too
But keep an eye on the stranger with the cave man shoe. . .!!

Jooblies, the Speedway and Best-Man-Fall
Too many good times to mention them all.
There's a lot of good people some gone, some remain,
Living elsewhere just isn't the same.

Whether it's Westcraigs, Stewart Milne, Wimpeys or Barratt
A hoose in "The Crescents" is 24 carat. . .!!
So, when you're next driving up Victoria Street,
You'll see why the Joneses' won't ever compete. . .!!

Mark Flynn

WHERE WOULD I BE. . . ?

If I could look out each morning
See the sun cast its rays on the river below.
If I could watch the moon at night
Reflecting its full splendour and glow.
If I could witness from this place
Changes of the seasons as they come and go.

If I could walk the fisherman's path
Along river bank near Livingstone's place.
If I could feel solitude, quiet and peace
Save startled wild cushie or deer like sounds.
If I could watch Heron on the Weir below
Or Salmon leaping to reach spawning ground.

If I could discover a Castle where many years past
Our Kinsmen fought for our independence and lost.
If I could explore carvings on red sandstone and lime
Where an artist called Hawkins devoted limitless time.
If I could live in the place where the Old Mill used to be
Where two thousand workers spun yarn for a fee.

If I could do all this where would I be?
I'd be home in Blantyre, that's where I'd be!
If I could do all this; who would I be?
If I could do all this. . . I would be me!

Andy Downie

THE DANDY

Ask anyone in Blantyre
Where is the Priory Plantation?
They'll hum and haw and hum again
For some form of explanation.

Ask them, "Where's The Dandy?
And a look comes o`er their face.
There's nobody Blantyre born
That doesn't know this place.

This dear green place of old
Lies on the Blantyre Braes,
Just along from where the Villager's
Used to bleach their claes.

In days of old a path was laid
From Hamilton down to Newton,
Thru` Blantir to the Pey Brig
Nuns Walk and Railway Station.

This path was made for workers
Who toiled in mill and mine,
And helped them get to work
By bridge or ferry on time.

In spring when hearts awakened
Throbbing in young breasts,
Down this path they would go
Dressed in their Sunday best.

From the Village to the Priory
Along this path they'd stroll,
To meet Laddies or Lassies
In the summer times of old.

So, if you've ever wondered
Or perhaps you've even guessed
This place was called The Dandy
Because of the way they dressed.

James Cornfield 2007

AN ODE TAE THE BLANEYS
1975-1982

Started at the Blaney's in August '75
It was the school that you went to before John Ogilvie High
The Headmaster, Mr O'Neil, a kind, good man was he,
But his secretary, Mrs Quigley, was as sweet as you can be!

Mrs Calpine was the infant weans school head
With hair jet black and nails all painted red!
Cross-country running was looked after by Miss Masterton
She immigrated to Spain, though, for a dream life in the sun!

Mrs Rea and Mrs Neilson, they were The Gorgeous Duo
More hats than a Milliner, more shoes than Jimmy Choo O!
Mr Golligly was in charge of the school's great football team
And the trophy's that they won were a sight to be seen.

The Inter School Sports, was THE event of the year
Mr McLaughlin prepped us well with teamwork and FEAR!
The 5 feeder schools were competing for the Trophy
The training was worthwhile cos to the Blaney's it was TOFFEE!

Playing "beat the belt" made you learn your 8-times table!
The Pope's visit to Scotland made school extra special.
Being first for Choir singing at Hamilton Town Hall
First Communion party in the school gym hall.

Sports day in the school was also a must
The parents all watching and causing a fuss.
Mrs Liddell taking charge of the girl's netball team
"Popeye" standing by selling dozens of ice cream!

School trips through the years were always great fun
Walking to Davy Livey's for all the P1's
An "Educational" visit to London was great,
Though the bus broke down and brought us back late!

Loch Lomond Bear Park, or a day out to Ayr
Culzean Castle, all the fun of the fair.
Mrs Callaghan always had time for her pupils
Concerts in the summer, Oklahoma the musical.

Mrs Welsh taking music for the silver Jubilee
Mr Harold, Mrs Sweeney and Mrs McGee.
Burst pipes in the winter and being sent home
Mr Savage the "janny" was always great fun.

Yes life at the Blaneys was more than just learning
Fun mixed with education, 7 years worth remembering.
It's no wonder the school has the best reputation.
And why I send my boy's there without hesitation!

Ann Crossar

BLANTIR WAY

I belong tae a wee toon called Blantyre
It rests in the county of Lanarkshire.
It's a quiet, yet busy wee place
An yer always sure tae ken a face.

If you walk along the busy main street
You'll no be disappointed whoever you meet.
The Blantir folk are aye up fir a bleather
Rain, hail or snaw, whitever the weather.

Everybody here has a great sense of humour
This is the product and fruits of our labour.
Sure at times it has been tough
As every family has had it rough.

The laughs and the wind-ups are legendary
Like the guy who had a hump like a dromedary.
It comes fae the black faces o' the miners
They were aw brave an' some of Blantir's finest.

If like Alan Sugar you "Took It to Market"
The feedback would be "Wit a Racket!"
Am always proud and happy to say
"A wiz brought up the Blantir Way!"

Tom Slaven

BLANTYRE PRIORY

On Blantyre Craig on the River Clyde there stood a Holy Place,
Wherein the word of Christendom was preached in olden days.
A brotherhood of holy men came here in days of yore
To spread the word of God as was their chosen chore.

This Priory built by men of God is no longer in our midst,
But should you approach this holy place in the early morning mist,
The feeling of a presence is everywhere around
And seems to overwhelm as you tread this holy ground.

One spring morn' I made my way down thru' Blantyre Braes
And came upon a stranger camped in this holy place,
Sitting in the morning sun beside a small camp fire
Deep in concentration, meditation his desire.

Closed deep in thought he sat and never opened his eyes
Completely unaware as I quietly passed him by.
I was almost out of sight when I heard him hail me so,
"Wait, kind sir! I beg of you! There is something I wish to know."

"Ever since I came here, there is a feeling of something near,
Watching o'er every move I make, whilst in my heart strikes fear.
'Tis why I've stayed here overnight and lay in yonder bed,
With night, came dreams and sounds, that linger in my head."

"Pray tell, kind sir, what is this place, do you know its history ?
Who made the carvings on the rock? Do they tell a story?
'Tis said there is a tunnel, twixt yonder castle and here ?
And that a monk lies buried under each and every osier ?"

"'Tis true there was a priory here, of that there is no doubt,
The carvings, Tommy Hawkins, was the man who carved them out.
'Tis said a tunnel was discovered in the year of '45,
A monk buried every tree, not proven nor denied.

All these things I tell you maybe true yet maybe false,
No one lives to tell truth of these ancient holy walls."
"But be they fact or fiction, 'tis difficult to explain,
Our elders spoke in whispers, of a Priory and Friar William.

So stranger please be careful, as you tread this holy ground,
For you are in the presence of some monks of such renown."
"Tho' they be dead and gone now, even yet they still remain,
To remind us that our God is near and this be his domain!

James Cornfield 2002

ST. JOSEPH'S 1971-1978

While I was out walking the other day,
I watched a piece of my childhood being taken away.
I can still see my teacher I can still see me play,
As this great machine took "Room One" away.

Now that the school is being reduced to rubble,
I can recall the times when we got into trouble.
You were sent to Miss King if you were a pest,
Or up to Big Bones for six of the best.

Then as we moved on, right up the school,
There was Miss Toker and she was no fool.
I can still see stars as she fires the duster,
As the lassie in front ducked as it missed her.

Then there was Sam Clements, he really was great.
On a Monday we played football and he'd keep us in late.
He taught us general knowledge, and to obey the rules,
He gave us his wisdom and prepared us for big school.

Now that the school is past its sell-by date,
It'll hold great memories for me and my classmates.
The tears, the laughter, the joy and the pain,
There's one thing for sure, you'll not get them back again.

The biggest school in Blantyre has come to its end,
For fifty five years it's been a parochial friend.
From nursery to secondary it's served the town well,
A saddening will fall upon us when we hear that last "BELL".

A new school is dawning and we all have with hopes.
But gone are the days of fitba and skipping ropes.
A new chapter is beginning, and the new school will emerge,
Let's hope our memories stay and never submerge.

J.J. Whelan

THE VILLAGE PEOPLE

When I was little, doon tae ma Granny Lynch's
Staring oot the windae , watching the finches.
"There's a big spoon, away and dig the gairden!"
It was a busy hoose, loud an full o fair maidens.

Ma Mam had six sisters and only wan brither.
They wur aw close and looked efter wan anither.
Liza, Mary, Frances, Bridget,
Margaret, Cathy, Ann & Tommy an'
Ma Granny Maggie was their proud Mammy.

Big Meg Hughes, she lived up the stair,
A nurse to trade, an treated all with care.
The times for many didn't go with ease
But we'd just sing oor songs an' shoot the breeze.

Tattie peelins, tae feed Connolly's pigs,
Then Connolly's Building lookin' fur digs.
Hours of fun an' laughter in the auld swing park.
Words o' warning- "Be hame afore dark!"

The Ulva Building and Tommy Morgan's Shoap.
Doon the Clyde swimming or a belly flop.
Across the road was the Village Bar
Where the men went if they fancied a jar.

Who were aw these strangers on the big bus?
We'd wave at them and they'd wave at us.
Where were they going? Davy Livvies, I presume.
Were did they come fae? Maybe Khartoum!

The days in The Village, are etched in my mind
I always say, "The Villagers are one of a kind!"
The honest Village People are a rare breed
Their lesson for life? "Enjoy but take heed!"

Tom Slaven

OOR AIN PARK

The joggers jog
Talkers talk
The pushchairs push
The walkers walk.

Stars of the future
Asleep in their pram
Proudly watched over
By mother and gran.

The old lady scatters
The bread on the ground
The hungry birds eat
With not a sound.

It's Sunday morning
Alone in the park
The vagabond figures
Been here since dark.

Less fortunate people
With sticks and chairs
We ask for a cure
Through forgiveness and prayers.

Dog walkers arrive
With family and friends
Volumes turned up
Enjoyment descends.

Time to go...

Drew Semple

THE CALL OF GREENHALL

Behind its auld wall its trees still stand tall
The auld path still leads doon tae the Cauther.
And ye kin walk here aw day, ye don't have tae pay
An'ye don't get wan bit o' bother.

Sometimes ah'll no meet a soul as ah go fur a stroll
An' sometimes that's the way ah like it,
An' ah pick up a stane an' ah take ma aim
And then that stane, ah skite it.

Here on fallen tree with poetry book
Ah kin read the works of Rupert Brooke.
Who takes me back tae another time,
Ah Grantchester - it sounds divine.

But this is the place ah love tae be
When nature runs unkempt and free.
Far from life and all its toils
A place man has yet to spoil.

By the Cauther's banks ye kin give the Lord thanks
Wae him ye hiv a guid talk tae
Wae him ye can share what ye think is unfair
Then wae him, ye can hiv a guid walk wae.

One day when my life is over
When I leave life's rushing river.
I hope God has a place like this
Where I can walk forever. . .

Brian Cummiskey

PETER CRAIG'S

Fur aw you folk fae Blantyre
Who've ventured near and far.
Ah wonder if ye remember
Long before we hid Spar.

There wis a wee butcher shoap
That sat oan the auld Main Street.
Wae its windie always shining
And full o' first class meats.

Wae its flair all full o' sawdust
And carcasses oan the racks.
They came from miles a'roon tae sample it
They even came in packs.

Some were waiting in the queue
Fur the Sunday roast,
Others they were waiting fur
Potted heid fur toast.

That wee red faced man that served ye
Well he was always nice.
Fur he knew whit you were waiting fur.
Wis "PETER CRAIG'S" finest square slice.

J.J. Whelan

LOS CRESENTOS

Every game was Lisbon in the Swingy Park,
Jumpers down for goal posts, headers in the dark.
Long before Asda, fancy phones and skittles
Your only two options were Cathy's or Little's.

We had auld Mr Rankin, Grandmaster of bowlin'
Who didn't laugh much when his club's bar got stolen.
He called in Big McKenzie, always one to crack the case.
The drop was Meechan`s gairden, it was gone without a trace.

Inventing entertainment was most nights of the week.
"Don't go past the post box!" was the rule of hide-and-seek.
A Winch in Dinsmore's doorway, split an oyster off the Tally,
Save my skins from Roxy's, then down Rascalz for a swally.

Toast the bards fae Blantir for their poems and their rhymes
Donate a quid to charity when you read the last two lines.
Thanks to Jimmy Whelan, Frank Devine and Thomas Slaven
And to all who went that extra mile with donations to The Haven.

Wan o The Flynns

THE HOUSE BY THE MILL IN THE MEADOW

Down Pech Brae by Calder's stream,
In autumn is a place so green.
Orange, gold and yellow too,
All enhanced by old Millheugh.
The place that Blantyre people know,
As 'The House by the Mill in the Meadow'
To describe the scene the poets unable,
methinks t'would need, John Constable.

Fact and fiction in this village abound,
Of tales untold of this ancient ground,
Wherein this house of old Millheugh,
Lived the Millar family everyone knew.
For 400 years they reigned supreme,
Lairds of all this pleasant scene,
Notable house guests came there daily,
Like Bothwell poetess, Joanna Baillie.

O'er yonder brig lies Malcolmwood,
A farm which straddles this ancient road.
Mary Queen of Scots and her gallant side,
On their way to battle at Langside.
And crossing the Calder at Pattenholm Ford,
This unruly warlike horde,
Camped yestreen in Dykesholm dell,
And drank of the water, from yonder well.

This army under Mary's command,
Well used to living off the land,
Partook of Farmer Rochead's cattle,
To sustain themselves for the morn's battle.
They ate, drank and then made merry,
With pillaged beef and mulled sherry.
Before they left and made their way,
to fate and destiny. . .

This ancient highway that they trod,
'Twas once the old stagecoach road
Thru' Blantyre from east and west,
With horses changed at the 'Hoolet's Nest.'
The Barnhill-Tavern- its proper name,
Is most indeed a place of fame-
Blanytre's oldest Tavern it maybe,
Being next to Aggie Bains house of 1563.

'Twas in this ancient part of town,
The rest o' Blantir was built around.
A Church stood here in days of yore,
Built by Monks from a distant shore.
An Iron Age burial urn was found,
Buried 'neath the marshy ground
Of Archer's Croft, where men honed their skills,
With bow and arrows and with quills.
A man of vision then came here,
And dammed the Clyde at yonder Weir.

David Dale used this stream,
For power to drive and fulfil his dream
To build a model village here,
And made houses, school and mills appear,
In Blantyre Works Village, his desire,
Then called this new place, Low Blantyre.

James Cornfield 2004

OWED TO FACEBOOK

A lot has been said of the woe of the 'Net
The bad it does to cause regret.
Communications way out of line
"A scourge on society of our time".

But where bad dwells good comes too
In forms that we never knew.
Facebook can be used in a positive way
To support good causes and have our say.

A town like Blantyre has known recent tears
But folk came together to comfort each other's fears.
Facebook got Blantyre to sit up and talk
To build this community on a more solid rock.

People from the past have reunited
And made other friends who have been invited.
Many women took part in a charity hike
We have danced together at the fabulous Soul Night.

Now good men have joined to publish rhymes
About Blantyre and all the good times.
A group emerged called Changing Places
Encouraging Blantyre stories and familiar faces.

This collective work will become a book
From which the proceeds and all money took
And donations made to publish too
Will all go to The Haven for the great work they do.

So the moral of this Facebook tale
Is that when there is enough good, then bad will fail.
The core of our community is full of grace
And Facebook has helped Blantyre show that wonderful face.

Arlene McWilliam Green

The Price of Coal

Liam Burgess

THE PRICE OF COAL

The sound of heavy pit boots marchin' up the street
Wis better that ony alarm cloak tae git me oan ma feet.
Anither day is startit and little did a ken
The sorrow this day wid bring afore the cloak struck ten.

The weans a` ready fur the school oan this wet an` windy morn.
A went tae the door tae see them awa` when I heard the dreaded horn.
Ma mither rushed oot past me, her face wis filled wi` fear
The horn wis blastin` louder, blood wis rushin` in ma ear.

Rushin` tae the pit-heid, trippin o`er the stanes,
Eveybody runnin`, some trailin` alang their weans.
Silence when we reached it, a tear at every e`e,
Wringin` hauns an` prayin, "God, please, yiv goat tae hear wur plea!".

They're bringin` up mair boadies, the number's noo a hunnner an` ten
Everybody's watchin` hopin` the faces they'll no ken.
Don't let it be my faither or ma wee brither Drew
He never wantit tae go doon the pit, bit joabs they wur few.

Through the crowd a heard a soun` o` ma mither sorely cryin`
A pushed an` shoved tae reach her, through the deid an' the dyin`.
Ma faither wis lyin` lifeless, never tae speak again.
He must have suffered terrible, bit noo he's free frae pain.

We didnae hive tae wait long afore we goat mair news.
They`ve noo brocht up ma brither, we knew him by his shoes.
Oh God, ye wurnae listenin` an a feel so sick wi` rage`!
Oor Drew wis only just a wean – thirteen years of age.

Wull someone tell my why whit happened doon that pit?
Some bloody thing went bang, wull someone tell me whit?
An` whit of a` the boadies still doon in that black hole?
Whit a price we've hud tae pey the day, whit a bloody price fur coal.

Etta Morrison (Gray) Born at 1 Dixon Street, Dixons Rows, Blantyre

EACH BING A HEADSTONE, EACH BING A TOMB

In Memory of My Father, Manus Duddy (1878 – 1926)

Inhuman the toil, inhuman the toll,
Our forbears endured, for the production of coal.
Their masters, the wealthy despots of old,
Sought maximum gain, from nature's black gold.
Scant was the care and scrimpy the wage,
For ill-fated Colliers, in that callous age.

By the Acts of Parliament, over the years,
Were miners enslaved, by legal gears.
Bound to the master, bound to the mine,
And their families too, by Arlings fine.
Crouched and crushed, in the bowels of the earth,
There was no pleasure, there was no mirth.

Mounds of Slag are all around.
Symbols of Serfdom, underground.
Symbols blood, sweat and tears,
Symbols of sacrifice, through countless years.
Grim and foreboding, like ominous doom
Each Bing a Headstone, each Bing a Tomb. . .

Elizabeth Duddy Parry

Manus Duddy, was born in 1878, in Co. Donegal, Ireland and came to Blantyre aged 18 to join his brothers, James and Michael, who were employed at Auchinraith Colliery and lived in the Colliery houses at Merry Rows. Whilst living with one of his brother's family, Manus obtained work at the colliery beside them. Manus was appalled at the cruel, inhumane working conditions and low wages of his fellow Colliers and began to take an interest in the newly-formed Miners Union. Unknown to others, he had a natural flair for negotiation and politics of that period. So much so, that in a very short period he was a member of the Miners Union as well as the Parish and County Councils and was also made Justice of the Peace. Such was his concern that he chose to work constant night shift (6 nights per week) at the Colliery, which enabled him to attend all the meetings of these committees which normally took place in the daytime and evenings. The constant strain of working, attending and travelling by train to these meetings over the years proved too much for Manus. Indeed, his close friends thought that it was the heavy work load that caused his early demise at the age of 48. In 1926, the very same year he had been chosen as an MP candidate elect of the Labour Party. The above poem was written by his daughter Elizabeth, whilst his Grandson, Charlie McGuire managed , after a long battle, to have the name “Manus Duddy Court” in the Thornhill Avenue, to perpetuate his grandfather’s name.

In this day and age, when allegations of corruption, fraud and bribery are made against MPs, Elected Officials, Bank Managers etc, it is my pleasure to write about a man who cared nought about fortune or fame, but simply the improvement of his fellow man. “To lay down your life for others”, springs to mind, as I acknowledge Manus and people like him.

James Cornfield 2007

THE RAPPER-UP MAN

In days gone by in the miners' rows
There lived a man who always rose
At an early hour from slumber deep
To waken miners from their sleep,
By rapping on the window pane,
No-matter the weather, wind or rain,
Be it Wullie, Mick or Dan
He was always known as the Rapper-up Man.

Now Dixon's Rows had such a man
But never called him the Rapper-up Man.
Not for them this common name
They had one of greater fame.
'The Sheriff' was by reputation
Their choice to waken up the nation.
To this grand title he had the honour
Of being the biggest 'Polis informer.'

'Tis said that when he was but eleven
He went down the pit to earn a living.
Into the darkness of the mine,
In the cage he was heard to whine,
'Faither dear, please take me hame!
Ah don't want tae go doon again!
It's nae fit place fur beast nor man,
Ah'd raither be a Rapper-up-man!'

Dressed like the Collier he longed to be
Moleskin trousers tied at the knee,
Eight pieced bunnet, old tweed coat,
Muffler tied in a hot pea knot.
In tackety boots he would stray,
The light from his Lantern showing the way,
'Roon all of Dixon's Collier houses,
Where he knew the names of all the spouses.

Rapping at the window you'd hear him cry,
'Wake up wifie! The time is nigh,
tae wake your men up now,
If they want to catch the very first tow.
Fur if they don't, ah'm no tae blame,
If they ur late and sent back hame, again!
Ah dae ma joab the best ah can,
Fur ah'm The Sheriff, yir Rapper-up Man!

Then one dark October morn,
Blantyre and Sheriff heard the pit horn,
Blasting out loud time after time,
The signal of trouble down in the mine.
Leaping out of bed into his clothes,
He made his way down through the Rows,
And wi' hundreds of others ran to the pithead,
To hear that 240 colliers were dead.

With tears in his eyes, he heard the roll call,
And uttered a silent prayer for all,
To any God who would listen to him,
Who could be heard above the din,
Of the wailing voices of mining folk,
Crying because their hearts were broke.
Their pain and suffering he'd remember,
Etched in his heart forever and ever.

The shout went up for volunteers,
And the Sheriff seemed tae lose his fears.
His hawn went up as fast as the others,
Amidst this band of collier brothers.
They're a funny crowd this collier breed,
Who risk their lives for others in need,
And with this only thought in mind,
Every man volunteered to go down the mine.

That day changed Blantyre for evermore,
When it brought trouble to every door.

In every house that you passed by,
You were sure to hear the woeful cry,
Of women folk in their But and Ben,
Mourning for their poor men.
These men and boys who would never come hame,
Back tae the Raws ever again.

But that day the Sheriff became a man,
With his father's pick and shovel in hand,
He toiled hard besides the others,
Tae try and save his collier brothers.
'Not fit for beast or man' he'd said,
True Colliers are born, they cannot be made.

This day would last in the hearts of all,
For those who go down to dig for coal!

James Cornfield 2004

Liam Burgess

SPIRIT AMONG THE FLAME

The day a black cloud descended on our town
The explosion brought pits two and three down.
For some, Dixons Colliery was to be their tomb
That day in October when the miners met their doom.

Twenty second of October Eighteen Seventy Seven
The day Blantir's brave colliers aw' went tae heaven.
Amongst the panic, explosion and the flames
Desperate screams to their maker, "Someone's to blame!"

The dreaded, pungent smell of firedamp all around
As these brave miners went to dig underground.
"Haw foreman, sumthin's no right doon there!"
"Aw haud yer weeshed! Ah dinnae care!"

As the clock ticked by and struck eight forty-five
A massive explosion, few did survive.
They left behind their wives and their children
Who knew only too well the sound of the siren.

The good people from Blantyre and other areas
Volunteered to help among the crying and hysteria.
Digging frantically to help save a man's a life,
To return to his weans and his distraught wife.

It took over a week to clear Dixon's Pit
And the people from Blantyre, all did their bit.
This town has spirit that can never be tamed
Even on the day we'd to put out the flame.

Tom Slaven 2011

A BREED APART

There was nothing romantic about coal mining
Jist a life of bloody toil.
Jist a life of hard labour
Underneath Scottish soil.

There was nothing romantic about coal mining
And miners got scant reward,
While coal-hearted bastards
Dined and gave thanks tae the Lord.

No, there wis nae romance in coal mining
Nor in any mining book a've read.
Jist a long list of names
Of the injured and the dead.

Brian Cummiskey 2008

COLLIERS EVERY WAN

(In memory of the Blantyre Disaster, 22nd October 1877)

Ah' wis born in the Raws a long time ago, in the hoose o' a Collier, ma' Faither ye'll know.
John Cornfield his name, this Faither o' mine, Mairrit ma Mither in days o' lang syne.

Tressa McGuigan fae the Spittal she came, tae Blantir tae mairry an' change her name.
Her faither's a Collier the same as her man, in fact, we're aw' Colliers, every wan.

They came fae Erin this family o' mine, tae Scotia's fair land tae work underground.
Wi' promise o' plenty ringin' in thur ears, they fun' only poverty, blood, sweat an' tears.

In Dixons Raws they settled doon, wi' Grannies an' Grandas aw' aroon.
Hunners o' Cousins ,Uncles an' Aunts, tho' times wur hard naebody'd waant.

Hard tho' the toil they worked wi' a will, wi' plenty o' bellies an' mooths tae fill.
Tae put bread oan the table an' coal oan the fire, tae leave hard time ahint, thur only desire.

Nothing hid changed at the end o' the day, same bosses, same serfdom, same low pay.
The local Scotchmen didnae like them at aw, fur they took aw' thur joabs an' thur hooses in the Raw.

Different religions didnae help them as well, in fact it wis jist like livin' in Hell.
Trouble in Pit, mair when they came hame, thur wir times when they wished they'd never came.

But aw' this wid change wi' the passage o' time, when fate took a hand doon there in that mine.
A build up o' gas , a wee naked flame, an' maist o' these colliers wid never go hame.

The horn oan the Pithead blew long an' forlorn, tae signal bad news that fateful morn.
Folk came runnin' fae aw' o'er the toon, every wan tae a man,volunteered tae go doon.

Nae thought o' danger, nor religion too, they aw' worked thegither wi' a common view.
The fellowship o' man wis born that day, in Blantir toon, how I wished it wid stay.

Two hundred and sixteen colliers lay dead , killed in pursuit o' thur dailly bread.
Men, Boys an' Uncles, Brither's an' aw', wid never return tae thur hoose in the Raw

Three men an' three boys, fae this family o' mine, aw' lost thur lives doon there in that mine.
Thur Wives an' Mither's, Agnes, Helen an' Jane, thur name wis Cornfield, the same as ma' ain. . .

Written in the Blantyre dialect.
James Cornfield 2002.

THIS COLLIER BREED

Within this band of Collier Brothers,
There sits a lad different from the others.
In the front row in his Tackety Bits,
Amidst Dixon's Collier's of 2 & 3 Pits.
Hands on knees, Glenny Lamp in between
Among his kin he's proud to be seen.
Just a boy of eleven like the rest of his mates
Doing a man's job for very poor rates.

He sits content amongst his neebors,
Ere going below to begin their labours.
Down the mine at the age of eleven,
These young boys went to earn a living.
These wee boys worked as hard as the men
Pushing full hutches, again and again.
From up the coal face towards the pit bottom
Just to make sure the "Cleek" wasn't stopping.

Down the coal mine afore daylight
They never came back up till it was night.
In summer they said it just seemed like fun
But in the dark of the winter, they never saw sun.
I look at this photo and feel very proud
Is my father John, amongst this crowd?
He and his father, went down these pits
Could he be the boy in the "Tackety Bits?"

I wonder. . .

James Cornfield – 2004

Heroes and Demons

Liam Burgess

THE BLANTYRE SAINT

This poem is dedicated to a Christian called John Graham
Who put his trust in Jesus Christ, our saviour bless his name.

A sinner like the rest of us, was destined for to burn
But he gave his heart to Jesus, and from his sins he'd turn.

At first he didn't know the truth, thought life could not be finer,
Then looking at nature's beauty thought, "Hey, a design must have a designer."

The lost souls on the streets today, it saddened John to see
So many on the sinful path, to a lost eternity.

So John then vowed unto Our Lord, that all who'd gone astray
He'd lead them to the glorious path, that one be saved each day.

So John's been on the Blantyre streets, how long? He can't remember.
Big Geordie says two hundred years and four months come December.

I'm sorry John, for my wee joke, believe me this is true
For the people you have helped, I really envy you.

Because all the angels up above, are all of one accord
For all the souls that you have led, to Jesus Christ their Lord.

John Graham (1899-1993) R.I.P.

Gerry McLaughlan 1987
(James Cornfield 2007)

THE WELFARE A.B.C

For forty years a Jewel in the crown
An institution within our town.
A community club for boxers to meet
To stand proud in victory and defeat.

Mc Dermott and Slaven, they're part of the team,
Coaching champions that is their dream.
Townsley, Clinton, Kelso and Campbell
To name but a few, on whom they've gambled.

Tuesdays and Fridays, the crew will be there
Punching bags with precision and care.
Training hard with sweat on their faces,
"Last Ten" the shout, as they pick up their paces.

Gloves on bags and skipping ropes
Courageous young men all with high hopes.
Boxing champs, all dreaming to be
Bobbing and weaving like the great "Ali".

Sparring with guys with well worn faces,
16oz gloves with yellow laces.
Fast and furious, punches go
Hitting the canvas, blow after blow.

Friday night the Grand Boxing Show
Approaching the ring, toe to toe.
Squaring up, for a good clean fight
Victory, the only prize of the night.

Cheering crowds as champs take their places
Fear and anguish upon their faces.
Cuts and bruises along the way
The Queensbury rules they all obey.

Discipline and respect are taught in this place
Restoring some faith in the human race.
Champion coaches who take great care
Training the future of "The Blantyre Welfare"

J.J. Whelan

IN THE FOOTSTEPS OF A GIANT

I always wanted to be just like him,
The man with the snow white hair,
In his big Arran sweater,
A friendly polar bear.

Always wanted to be just like him,
And now I think I can
Follow in giant footsteps,
Of a kind and loving Blantyre man.

Brian Cummiskey

THE WEE GOD

How wid ye like tae wield great power?
Dae ye fancy drinkin' efter hours?
Frequent visits tae foreign places?
Or get cheap bevvy by the cases?

How wid ye like tae command respect,
And huv folk know yer always correct?
Or fraternise wi' those in showbiz,
While tellin' them how hard your job is?

How aboot money, is that yer scene?
Nae problem, if ye know whit Ah mean;
Tae qualify for this employment,
Ye'll huv tae meet aw these requirements:

Ye must be quick-tempered efter a few,
Ye definitely must huv a low IQ,
And when there's trouble ye'll huv tae act,
(Ye don't need diplomacy or tact).

Yer uniform's a demob jaikit,
Tae round it aff ye must look glaikit,
And there's wan rule ye must remember,
"Make things hard for guests and members."

"Whit job can that be," Ah hear ye say,
"Surely there's naewan like that today?"
But there is, believe me, it's nae fluke,
Go tae ony social club and look.

Ye'll see these wee men, a special breed,
Ye can tell wan by his swollen heid,
And a wee badge pinned tae his lapel,
"Committee Man"... so behave yersel!

Lon McIlwraith

MR YUILL AND MR DODDS

While still a boy in St Joseph's school,
I learned my maths and writing.
I learned of Romans Emperors,
And of wars and heroic fighting.

As much as teachers taught us this,
And other odds 'n sods,
The things I learned most deeply then,
Were the curse words Yuill and Dodds.

They sent their trucks like Moscow's tanks,
To keep the Craig fires burning.
They obeyed their master in Number 10,
The devil who was not for turning.

The same she-devil who sent ma auld man,
From the tool room to the Broo.
The very same uncaring beast,
Who Yuill and Dodds did woo.

So Mr Yuill and Mr Dodds,
Your trucks still thunder on.
You may have smashed the miners,
But your souls have long since gone.

And when your names are heard today,
Some may just shrug their shoulders.
But still my hands are reaching for,
Rocks and stones and boulders.

James O'Donnelly

REFLECTIONS

As I gaze in this mirror what do I see?
An aged reflection staring back at me.
I can't help, but to stop and stare
Old Father Time has not been fair.

The face in this mirror resembles another.
Is it my Father or is it my Mother?
The face in the mirror now echoes the past
Like a glance, time is fleeting, ever so fast.

As I gaze in this mirror I tremble with fear
That the end of my time is drawing near.
But from this mirror I need not look away
To discover the man I am today. . .

J.J. Whelan

THE BOXER

You get the call, you've got a fight.
6 weeks today on the Friday night.
Must start training and get ready.
Dizzy with the rush, you need to keep steady.

You want to know your opponent's name
And do your homework, but it's all the same.
Cos, on fight night it's between you and him
And all the work you've done in the gym.

Up early mornings running the roads
Put on a back pack to heavy the load.
The roads are hard and the weather cold.
It doesn't get any easier, so I am told.

Running faster, faster, longer!
This will do well and make me stronger.
In the gym, skip, sparring, bags and pads,
Training hard with the other lads.

At last, fight night is finally here.
Focus, adrenalin and conquer your fear.
Into the arena, oh what a sight!
Hundreds of people to watch the fight.

Centre of the ring, stare into his eyes
Ref and officials all in their ties.
Keep his gaze, let him know you're there.
"Remember boys, you've got to fight fair!"

Back to your corner, further instruction.
Come out and fight. It's time for destruction.
Shouts of support ring in your ears.
Need to stay focused, fight back the tears.

You take the first punch and now you calm down
As the noise of the crowd starts to drown.
Feeling relaxed with your pounding heart racing
"Keep on jabbing and gie him a lacing!"

The fight is over and you've given your all.
Whatever the decision, you can stand tall.
Face is torn, bruised, battered and dazed
But the verdict is in and it's your arm that's raised.

Tom Slaven

THE METER BEATER

Blantyre is a funny wee place, wae awe its different folks,
There's people there who'd put Oxford and Cambridge to shame,
They've pulled so many strokes.
But there's wan wee man, I'll always remember,
When he came to read the meter
Wae his wee long coat and bunnet,
He was known as "THE METER BEATER".

Now there was the dreaded time every quarter, in the household year,
When they came to read yer meter,"Oh, and why was it so dear?
But if you knew the "METER BEATER" he'd fill yer heart with cheer,
Cause he was there the day before the meter man,
Tae turn it back fur the year.

Whether you were gas or electric he always had a way,
Always making sure he fixed it, so ye did'nae hift tae pay.
Now this wee man, he wis great, but only if he wis sober,
Fur if he got the numbers wrang in June,
You'd be living like October.
Sittin wae the heatin oan and windaes open at full mast,
Sweat runnin aff ye, cause he'd turned it back too fast.

There wis wan wee wummin who got caught,
Oh' whit a cryin shame.
Her light wis cut aff fur a fortnight,
As her family cooried 'roon a flame.
Now everybody in that scheme they were all the same,
But nae 'body would admit tae it, because of the dreaded shame.

Now I wonder if ye remember that wee man, fur he was always there,
Turning back yer meters and making sure life was fair,
But if the local polis, or the powers that reign above,
Ever thought aboot capturing him. . .?

J.J. Whelan

BRAW BROON

Braw Broon was ae a bonny lass,
A bonny lass, a bonny lass,
There's no nane lass could e'er surpass,
The bonny wee Braw Broon.

She called me for a lib'ry book,
I tried tae gie the fine a jook,
She made me pay, an' I was hooked,
By bonny wee Braw Broon.

Her mither said that I was bad,
Her faither ca'd me, twice, a cad,
I paid nae mind, 'cause I was glad,
Tae be wi' wee Braw Broon.

I showed her true I'm no nane rake,
Her bonny heart I widnae break,
Nae thing on earth could owertake,
My love for wee Braw Broon.

Noo aw these mony years huv passed,
She's still ma ain wee bonny lass,
We'll be together tae the last,
My bonny wee Braw Broon.

Lon McIlwraith

ANY SINGERS, ANY SONGS!

"Gei's a song!"
"Ach, no the noo!"
"Whit's wrang hen? That's no' like you."
"Ah'm jist no ready, ah canny think,
Mibbe ah need some mair tae drink."
"Gei hur annurrer", wis the command.
Then she'll sing tae beat the band.

Efter a few, poured withoot measure,
She said, "Cum oan noo, name yer pleasure!
Whit's it tae be? Ah'll sing whit ye want."
She wis confident, she could chant.

"Is it Rabbie, Shirley, or Lena Martell?"
This lassie wis said tae hiv a voice like a bell.
By this time people wur gettin' fed up wi' the patter.
"Fur guidness sake sing, it disny matter!"

"If she disny sing, ah'll no borra,
Ye see, ah'm up fur work the morra."
But the lassie finally did staun up,
Drinkin' Lanny fae a china cup.
Her song wis long, bit no' forgotten.
She could sing nane, she wis BLOODY ROTTEN!!!

Anon

FAT CATS

Arise at six thirty, shower and shave
Android state, such a way to behave.
Laptop in place, in its little black case
Awaiting the train, just another blank face.

Pinstripe suit and self-coloured tie,
Polished shoes and black hair dye.
A cup of coffee and the morning rag
Out in the rain an' having a fag.

Another high flyer in this City Place
Trying to keep up with the human race.
Mr. Jones got this, Mr. Jones got that
His life, depicted in a drab format.

Home to the wife, two kids and the dog,
Sit down and relax, another hard slog.
Never recalling what happened that day
For another's livelihood you grasped away.

Another day in this fearsome rat-race
Robbing the poor, such a disgrace.
Rewarding themselves with wads of cash
Blaming all others, as it came to a crash.

J. J. Whelan

The Demon Drink

Blantyre's oldest public house " The Barnhill Tavern"

THE BALLAD OF THE PALE RIDER

He stood there like a sentinel in the middle of the bar,
And something drew me to him and I offered him a jar.
But he refused my offer; he only shook his head,
And with a look to spook the Devil,
He fixed his gaze and said:
"Look around you kid; most of these men are dead,
And the ones that think they are living,
Have lives filled with fear and dread.
Some of them were once good men,
But that was long ago.
And some of them had souls as pure as driven snow.

For some men, drinking liquor gives them cancer of the soul,
And they try and fill the emptiness
But they just burn a bigger hole.
Some men can take it or leave it,
Some men can't leave it alone.
And that's why these men sitting here,
Are nowt but skin and bone.

Now, I ain't no preacher man, but the liquor's got a hold on you.
So give up now kid or you
Will join this motley crew.
And you should take it from me,
Don't you wait till that last bell,
Or you'll be standing here one night
As the sentinel from hell."

Brian Cummiskey
Inspired by Clint Eastwood
And a man I met in a pub.

BLANTYRE BOOZERS

The pubs in Blantyre all have changed,
Decor, names all rearranged.
How well are they all remembered?
Name which ones went up in embers.

The Auchinraith and Stanley too
Are gone but just to name a few.
These places from the distant years
Where folk stop by to sip their beers.

The Red Lion upon Stonefield Road
Is now a place where folk abode.
The town has changed so very fast
Wiping memories from Blantyre's past.

Caspers, Rascalz - take your pick
It really makes me feel quite sick.
That a once -bustling hostelry
Is now a public library!

Some of the old ones have survived
The ones some fools think are wee dives.
The Hoolits, Village and the Welly
A proper pub to fill yer belly.

No fancy menu, no choice of wine
Just regulars with their bookie's line.
Pubs with dugs, a rare old sight,
Are welcome there both day and night.

Why should I care, you may wonder why,
That these wee pubs need to survive.
Well just between you and me,
We're preserving Blantyre's history.

Michael O'Donnelly

BARS AND SUPERSTARS

Sunday morning and the smell of ham is travellin up the stair.
Can still taste last nite's bevy and pizza thro ma hair.
We set aboot oor Saturday nite, just the back of 8.
An' that was us till closing time, we ended in a state.

Two pints in the Parkville, the West End for a jar,
Then back to Craig's then the Cozy, or wiz it The Priory Bar?
The Smiddy it was timeless, the smell was in the air-
Fags and pipes and smelly dugs, wi sawdust on the flair.

Headin tae Matt Boyle`s, the crowd was pretty mixed.
Wi' the usual cry fae Big John, 'Haw,Wee man, how ur ye fixed?".
Andy Kelly is holdin court, with 'Burn your playhouse down'
Pipe Armstrong telling stories, the funniest guy in town.

The Village Bar, Teddies, the Knights or Union Jack.
We headed to the Hoolets, just to hear the crack.
We staggered past the Doon Inn, then staggered down to The Vics,
Then James McGuire shouted, 'hey boys am takin pics.'

All the pubs have changed now, and some are even gone.
The superstars in all the bars have passed their stories on.
At the height and in their heyday these guys were aw' the best
But sadly here no longer and mostly laid to rest.

Drew Semple

SUNDAY MORNING NIGHTMARE

Boozing away, drinking all night
Don't really care if you get into a fight.
Having great fun, going to great places
Tomorrow you'll move at very slow paces.

Its midday on Sunday and the rooms spinning round
You're under the covers not making a sound.
And you pray to God, the roller coaster will halt
Asking Him, "Is this really my fault?"

You analyse your food, now that's got you thinking
It must be that kebab, it's never my drinking.
It can't be the cider, the vodka and mix
It must be that donner, that's making me sick.

The sweating has started, your hearts started thumping,
You're starting to itch, and your body is jumping.
You're talking to God on that big white phone
Praying that the Devil will leave you alone.

You drift off to sleep and the nightmares begin.
The Devil is calling you, because you have sinned.
Then you start thinking, could this be the day
The "Big Man" is coming to take me away?

Then you're awake and you find it ironic
All you want to do is search for a tonic.
Two small tablets and a glass of Irn Bru
That's all that you needed, to really fix you.

A whole day is lost and nothing is gained
You can be thankful that you still remain.
You can only take heed and be forewarned
About that dreaded curse of "JOHN BARLEYCORN"

J.J. Whelan

COME JINE ME

Refresh yersel, come jine me do!
Come staun ower here and huv a few,
And we'll baith woo the golden grain,
Come jine me fur a hauf, my friend.

The influence is nice, ye'll see,
When under it yer worries flee,
And leave ye free, nae cares or pain,
There's two mair comin' up again.

So here's a toast tae your guid health!
Tae happiness and future wealth!
Onythin' else ye care tae name,
Guid on ye, get them up again.

Ah'm gled ye've came tae jine me here,
Tae share a hauf, perhaps a beer,
So Ah say cheers! Let's no' restrain!
Ah'd better order up again.

Whit dae ye think of this wee place?
A better pub ye couldnae trace,
Its friendly face has equal nane,
Ah think it's your turn, same again.

In pubs it's company they sell,
There's plenty folk just like yersel,
The bevvy well, mix wi' their ain,
Haud on, Ah'll get them up again.

Ah like a wee hauf noo and then,
In ony nummer up tae ten,
Ah'm sure ye ken, Ah could refrain,
It's time ye got them up again.

There's some folk say Ah drink too much,
They say fur me it's just a crutch,
Held in its clutch, gaun doon the drain,
Nonsense! Ah'll order up again!

Huv anither, Ah must insist,
Ye cannae leave until ye're pissed,
Ye'll no be missed, by them back hame,
Besides, it's your round, same again.

Drink up noo, don't dilly-dally,
Ye look a bit peely-wally,
Whit's the tally? Ma turn again?
We'll huv anither two the same.

Ye'd maybe better huv a brek,
Ye look ready tae hit the deck,
A bevvied wreck, ye're oot the game,
Fae noo on Ah'll just buy ma ain.

Whit possessed ye tae drink sae much?
Ye'd think it's yer first time, as such,
Right ootae touch, like some daft wean,
Haud on, Ah need a drink again.

Sit doon ower there and huv a rest,
Even though ye tried yer best,
Ye've failed the test, ye're no' a man,
Ye cannae haud it like Ah can.

Ach, never mind, ye'll be okay,
Ah drink in here near every day,
Ye're welcome tae jine me again,
Oh, by the way, whit's yer name?

Lon McIlwraith

THE BINGO BUNGLE

Ah've spent a lot of time in pubs,
And quite a bit in social clubs,
Like oor local Miners Welfare,
We had some rerr laughs drinkin' there.

There wis wan Sunday night, Ah think,
The crack wis guid, just like the drink,
While up on stage, gaun through her paces,
The cabaret, straight fae "New Faces".

Well, so said the poster on the wa',
The committee says that aboot them aw,
But even though she tried her best,
She sounded just like aw the rest.

And as she sang some wee love ballad,
Giving it aw the feeling she had,
A voice arose, just tae reward her,
"Right c'mon youse lot, best of order!"

Fairly soon it wis time fur the brek,
Time fur bingo, a pain in the neck,
When wise men leave, and go tae the bar,
Where they get peace tae huv a few jars.

But that night some of us stayed behind,
No' tae play bingo, that we declined,
But tae watch Auld Davie's hopeless plight,
As he read oot the nummers that night.

(That prestigious job, nummer wan,
Belonged tae the heid committee man,
But he wis absent, away tae Spain,
He said it wis club business, again.)

So there wis Auld Davie up on stage,
Crashin' aboot in a mad rampage,
Trippin' ower wires, an' knockin' things doon,
Tryin' tae make thae wee baws go roon.

Yet even as he near wrecked the place,
That confident look ne'er left his face,
And wance he finally got things right,
He toddled aff fur anither pint.

Ten mins later everywan's ready,
They've got their tickets and their bevvy,
Auld Davie steps up, confident still,
Grabs haud of the mike, and sterts doonhill:

"The furst gemme - haw whit's wrang wi' this?"
Nae sound fae the speakers, just a hiss,
Oot in the crowd you could hear the groans,
Then somewan shouted, "Switch it oan!"

Undaunted by this technical hitch,
He looked at the mike, and saw the switch,
He clicked it on, and a piercing screech,
Near blew everywan ootae their seats!

A wee committee man jumped on stage,
(That's quite a feat fur a man his age),
He went tae the amp, and twiddled some knobs,
Then turned tae Davie, and gied him the nod.

"Testing, wan, two, testing... Aye, that's fine,
Right, this furst gemme's fur a single line!"
The gemme wis on, and the heids were doon,
Auld Davie had us rollin' aroon:

"Ninety-nine, naw wait, that's sixty-six;
Next wan, fifty-six, go tae the flicks;
Diamond weddin', nummer forty;
This is ma wife's age, eight-oh, eighty."

He went on like that aw night long,
Makin' it up as he went along,
We aw thought it wis hilarious,
But no' Auld Davie, he wis serious!

The first three gemmes dragged on forever,
Fanatic players yapped together,
"Somethin's wrang", you could hear them whinin',
And afore long aw the others jined in.

Wan wee wuman, heidscarf and a fag,
Wi' ashtrays and glasses in her bag,
And markin' aff ten tickets at wance,
Yells oot, "Haw Davie, geeza chance!"

Well, soon the rabble were on their feet,
Wan wuman even stood on her seat,
"There's nummers missin', Ah want a check!"
"The gemme's a bogey!" - "Haw, geeza brek!"

The wee committee man grabbed the mike,
And shouted, "Ah've never seen the like!
Right, c'mon youse lot, sit doon will ye?
Noo Davie here's daein' his best fur ye!"

But his plea wis lost in the uproar,
"We want a check!" the rabble implored,
So reluctantly he said, "Awright!
We're gaunnae be here aw bloody night!"

They waited fur the baws tae come oot,
And maistae the crowd were in nae doot,
The two men's faces were gettin' red,
"We'll huv tae be careful," Davie said.

They didnae want tae start a panic,
Davie tried tae be diplomatic:
"They're aw there as far as Ah can see...
Except four, nineteen an' fifty-three."

Pandemonium then erupted!
The mob just aboot self-destructed!
A big fat wuman jumped up and doon,
And near cowped the tables aw aroon!

"That's no' fair!" she yells, makin' a scene,
"Ah've waitit ages fur that nineteen!
Ah want a prize, or ma money back!"
Whit she needed wis a brain attack.

And the winners didnae think it funny,
When somewan yelled, "Take back the money!"
"You'll be lucky, we've drank maistae it!
It's no' oor fault he made an arsae it!"

And that wee wuman, heidscarf and a fag,
Wi' ashtrays and glasses in her bag,
She stood there shoutin', wi' aw her heart,
"Ye never checked yer baws at the start!"

Well, it took a while tae calm the fools,
The gemme went on with modified rules,
But every time that "House!" wis shouted,
True tae form, an argument started.

The poor singer wondered whit wis wrang,
Naewan listened tae a word she sang,
The just continued the great debate,
While drinkin' themsels intae a state.

But though Auld Davie's nerves were shattered,
He got free drink, that's aw that mattered,
And he knew somethin', but dared no speak,
He wis callin' the bingo, all week!

Lon McIlwraith

A STAGGER ROON BLANTIR

From "Auld Auchinraith Club"
It's No Very Far
Across The Road
To "Kelly's Bar".
A Pint In There
Then Ow'r Tae "The Livingstone
Then It's Up The Road
And intae "The Wellington".
The Sloap Oan The Flair
Made Ye Feel Quite Giddy
So It's doon The Road
And On Tae "The Smiddy"
Fur Anither Jar
Then Off Again
Tae "The Priory Bar".
Ah Nearly forgoat
"The Castle Vaults"
Ye Come Oot O' There
Dain Summersaults!
A Game O' Darts
Wi' Wee Tam Horner
Then Aff Ah Went
Tae "The Cosy Corner"
After a Pint in "The Central"
Ah Wiz Tapped Fur The Reddies
An'Half An Hour Later
Ah Wiz In "Big Teddies".
Someone Farted
A Terrible Smell
So Ah Boddy Swerved
Tae "The Parkville Hotel".
A Hauf In There
An Anither Jar
Then Doon The Road
Tae "The West End Bar"

Efter A Walk
Yur Due A Rest
So Ah Jist Drapped In
Tae "The Hoolet's Nest"
A Game O' Dominoes
Wi' Awe Yir Pals
Then Oot Fur A Walk
And Intae "Vals"
A Pint in There
And Ah'm Oan Ma Knees
So Ah Jist Crawled Owr
Tae "Auld J.B.'s"
Two Ta Go
So Haud Yur Piles
There's Only "Blakely's"
And "Matt Biles".
Ah Went Intae "The Doon Inn"
Oan Ma Way Hame
Then Intae "The Commercial"
Tae See An Auld Flame.
But The Flame Wiz Oot
So Ah Got A Lift In A Car
And Landed In "The Village Bar"

Ah Never Mentioned
"The Livery Hotel"
Or Awe The Clubs
And Bars as well

But Ah'll Dae That The Morra. . .
. . .When Ah'm Oot Fur A Lager
A Good Excuse. . .
. . .Fur Anither
. . .Stagger.

Anon.

A Sense of Loss

Liam Burgess

TO REMINISCE

I thought I saw you the other day.
I was mistaken, yet, strange to say,
I thought that I could sense you near
Again, mistaken, maybe through fear,

I feel I can reach out and touch you
But you're not there and it hurts to
Sometimes think we are sitting together
Then realise, you're not here, gone forever.

If only we could have another chance
Just one last chat or maybe a dance.
I'll always remember the way we were
Unconditional, loyal and always there.

Only half a chance to say goodbye
That still hurts and makes me cry-
The emotion is raw and everlasting of
The day when I learned of your passing.

I thought I heard you earlier today
Maybe subconscious but I heard you say,
"C'mon be strong and follow your faith
Always remember we don't die in death."

Only just yesterday, I caught your stare
Then I remembered, you're not there.
If only we'd one chance to reminisce.
The times with you both are what I miss.

Tom Slaven

FAITH

Through an elegant entrance we walk
To an ageing pew we flock.
We come to pray and to weep
Another friend gone to sleep.

Eyes fixed on God's own vendor
Depicting stories with such splendour.
Voices raised to the church's heights
His message spread with soulful delight.

Stained glass in all its grace
Beam prisms of colours on open space.
Candles and statues, proud in presence
Beautiful flowers, vibrant in fragrance.

Fore the altar, a casket of wood
Daunting aura around it stood.
Sprinkled with water, now been blessed
Final commendation, odour of incense.

The crucifix hangs on the wall
Reflecting a son who died for us all.
Satan tempts us to give in.
Will our Faith stay strong within?

J.J. Whelan

WITH THE BRIM OF MY HAT TURNED DOWN

I glanced and you looked away. . .
To get your attention, I said words
I once heard Humphrey Bogart say,
Like, "Here's looking at you kid
You're a swell looking Dame",
But the words just skittled out
The bar room door at your back
Onto the Black and White Streets.
And all my lexis of desire
Pulverised with your last icy look of disdain.
Yet I did my best and no one
Will ever convince me
We couldn't have been
Fantastic lovers. . .

Marian Cummiskey Kane

Reamonn Gormley R.I.P.

THE LAST SONG OF THE LARK

As the winter sun fades to grey
And the brightest star steals away,
The howling wind thrashes around
And thunderous rain engulfs the ground.
No autumn leaves upon the lawn,
No flowers blooming in the early dawn.
Apple blossom petals nowhere to be found
As the noise of silence is the only sound.
Today another young man has gone
And the beautiful lark has lost her song

Paul Murray

AMERICAN DREAM?

Here am I, a proud Kerry man
I travelled here to see your fine land.
I took to the road, started laying your tracks
Building your bridges and climbing the stacks.

They'd call me Paddy or sometimes Mick
I'd always be there taking some stick.
I was the policeman who pounded the beat
Keeping the bad guys off your streets.

As generations pass, times evolve
Congress changing, many problems to solve.
Towers come tumbling, a country on its knees
Young men sent to war, in hope to appease.

My only son deployed to the front line
Slain by the Afghans in such a short time.
A great soccer coach destined was he
An Irish American hero forever will be.

I campaign for justice that this war should stop
To stop bringing young men home in a box
I often wonder how life would be
If I'd never chased the dream in "The Land of the Free."

J.J. Whelan

FOREVER IN MY MIND

When I think of you
It always makes me smile
Although I know that I won't see you for a while.
There are still times when I get sad
But most of all I'm glad,
So glad of all the sweet times that we had.

When I see you I want to touch you're perfect face
And then you look at me and you brighten up my day.
You're laughter fills the air
There is nothing that can compare to
The way I feel about you Every day.

Every breath I take will bring me close to you,
Every tear I cry, I cry for you.
But what I know for sure,
You're 'forever in my mind'
And I know that you are with me all the time.

Andy Downie

GUARDIAN ANGEL

In the dark of night he appeared to me
At the end of my bed for me to see.
Snow white hair and enchanting smile
He sat and talked, for a little while.

(DO NOT BE AFRAID)

He told me things from beyond the grave
Why people pass for others to be saved.
My parents are happy and together again
Brother Alex, at peace with his friends.

(DO NOT BE AFRAID)

I take great comfort from what he said
Released a lot from my subconscious head.
My Guardian Angel from the deep abyss
Watching over the souls of those I miss.

(DO NOT BE AFRAID)

J.J. Whelan

SEASONS

You're gone now.
And to apportion no blame
I must move away from a time
That knows all of my thoughts.
In this time of renewal I will stay
In limbo until the hesitant leaves drift,
Awaiting autumn skirmishes
Until I melt into mellowing mists
Injecting me with the absolute remnants
Of old joys, as I ingest the last blaze of our
Last summer. . . and let the hours ache.

Marion Cummiskey Kane

ABSENT FRIENDS

When I stare upon this vacant chair
I often wonder why you're not there.
When I look upon the empty glass
I recall great memories of the past.

A certain phrase or song you'd sing
Fond memories come flooding in.
A funny line or a certain smile
It makes me pause and think a while.

I often think of times gone by
Look up to God and ask him "Why?"
It was your time to be called away.
They say he works in mysterious ways.

So now you've taken leave of life
You're on your journey to a better life.
To a place with harps, where angels sing
And you'll sit beneath their wings.

J.J. Whelan
In memory of a dear friend, Gary Miller 1963 – 2007.

Changing Places 2

Hordes along Main Street
In protest at the knife.
Outcries and meetings
And grief for lost life.

Standing united
Against mindless Neds,
Determined our weans
Will sleep safe in their beds.

J.J. Whelan

This truly fantastic anthology of verse would never have seen the light of day were it not for the outstanding assistance received from countless individuals, groups and organisations who have provided *Changing Places* with finance, moral support and encouragement over this past 8 months.

Of course for the editorial board of *Changing Places* it has been a labour of love to have been involved in such a worthwhile project. How do we go about thanking the numerous individuals and bodies who have assisted in bringing this project to fruition? We are of the opinion that it would be unfair to single out any particular individual/organisation in terms of the size of donation. All financial donations, no matter how large or small, played a part in bringing this work to print.

Changing Places would like to thank each and every single person who has assisted us in this project. We have listed all those in alphabetical order below and hope you will all take this as an indication of the gratitude we extend towards you for your sterling support.

Frank Devine, Tom Slaven & Jimmy Whelan, 2nd September 2011.

Acknowledgements :

Abigail Duffy Mullins
Alan Baird
Alexander Henderson
Alexandria Shaw
Alister Mathieson
Andrew Burton
Andrew McLachlan
Andy Paterson
Anne Anderson
Ann and Ian Crossar
Ann Marie Lappin
Baby Grace Tierney
Bernadette McParland
Bernadette Rooney
Blantyre Walk 'N' Rollers
Brian Reid
Cahal and Eamonn Whelan
Carol and Eddie Pollock
Carol Tierney
Carole De Placido
Carole Moran
Catherine Maider
Christine Robertson
Claire Clinton
Clare Woods
Colin King
Colin Stewart
Cornfield Family
Cummiskey Family
Danny Scully
Dave Stuart
David Forrest
Denise Talent
Douglas Gordon

Drew Semple
Eddie Morrison (Headmaster JOHS)
Eddie O'Donnelly
Edith Bulloch
Elaine McInally
Elaine McQuade
Elaine McQuade Petriat
Elaine Veitch
Eleanor Rodgers Cummiskey
Elizabeth Daly
Elizabeth Martin
Elizabeth McQuade Semple
Erin Catherine Slaven
Erin Devine
Fairlie Gordon
Finbar Francis Bryson
Fiona O'Brien
Frances Burns
Frances Hutcheson
Gary Doonin
Gary Nelson
Gary Stewart
Gerard O'Donnelly
Gerard Summers
Gerry and Nancy Kelly
George Cairns
George McGinty
Gordon Fortheringham
Gormley Family
Harry Hood and all at the Parkville, Blantyre
Harry Smith and Family
Helen McGowan Munday
Helen Stewart
Honey Semple
Hugh and Kathleen Nelson
Hughes Health and Fitness (Blantyre)
Ian Lappin
Ian Craig and Family
Isabel McLean
Isabel Williamson
Isabella Frostrick
Isabel Boyle Williams
Jacqueline O'Donnelly
Jan Olaf and Carolyn Mikkelsen
James B. Brown
James Connor
James O'Donnelly
James White
Janette Stewart
Janice and Jacqueline Lynch
JDS (Blantyre)
Jean Miller
Jean Morrison
Jean Nicol
Jeanette McLaughlin
Jess Toprak
Jill Walsh
Jim and Christine Donnelly
Jim Brankin
Jimmy and Peggy (Carabine) Rooney
John and Anne Marie Murray
John Carrigans (Blantyre)
John Carrigans (Eddlewood)
John Daly
John Flynn
John Gerard and Eleanor Wemyss
John McQuade
John Ogilvie High School
John Woodhouse
Johnny and Dominic Crossar
John Pollock
John Semple
Julie Hailstones
Karen Devine
Karen Glen
Karen McDade
Karen Slaven
Kenny Downie
Kerry O'Donnelly

Kerry Summers
Kerry Toner
Kevin O'Hara
Kevin O'Neil
Laura Gaddis
Lesley Logan
L.M. Madden
Lilian McGinty
Linda O'Donnell
Lisa Duffy
Liz and John McGinty
Liz Clelland
Liz Daley
Liz Doonin
Liz Semple
Lon McIlWraith
Lorraine Pearson
Louise McAleer
Lynda Oughton
Lynn Kelly
Lynne Derby
Lynne Lappin
Marc and Ellie McDonald
Margaret Allan
Margaret Reilly McGinley
Marion Boyle Barnes
Marion Robertson
Mark Logan
Martin Mahony
Mary Anne Poneszkis
Mary Cameron
Mary McGuire
Mary Mullen
Mary Summers
Maureen Donnelly
Maureen Friery Moran
May Cocozza
Michael O'Donnelly
Michael and Patrick McGowan
Michele Milligan
Monica Whelan
Morag Ravenscroft
Myra Dolan
Nancy and Jimmy Flynn
Norma Foley
Olivia Lea Donaghy
Pat Oliver
Patrick Slaven
Patricia Cunningham
Paul Lafferty
Paul Veverka
Rena O'Donnell
Reid The Printers (Blantyre)
Robert Crothers (Crum)
Roberta Stewart
Rose Kellachan
Ross Hyslop
Sadie Dolan
Sal O'Neil
Sarah and Louise O'Neill
Sarah Sked
Scott Moore
Seosamh O'Glacain (Joe Glackin)
Sharon Callaghan
Sharon Doonin
Sharon Kyle
Sheila Strang
Stephen Murray
Stephen Pillans
Stevie McKnight
Shirley Fallon
Teresa Brannan
Terry Fox
Thomas and Antoinette Barratt
Tom Whelan and Family
Yvonne Shaw
Worldmark Int. Ltd.